WEATHE
THE GRIEF
STORM

WEATHERING THE GRIEF STORM

LEARNING TO THRIVE WITHIN LOSS

JULIE KICK

Requests for permission to make copies of any part of the work should be sent to the following email: Julie@weatheringthegriefstorm.com

Published and distributed by Merack Publishing.
Library of Congress Control Number: 2021904942
Kick, Julie, 1963-
Weathering the Grief Storm: Learning To THRIVE Within Loss

Paperback: ISBN 978-1-949635-90-4
eBook: ISBN 978-1-949635-91-1
Hardcover: ISBN 978-1-949635-92-8

DEDICATION

For my beloved John, who came into my life at the perfect time, exited it far too soon, and taught me how I was supposed to be loved while you were here. You weren't perfect, but you were perfect for me. I will always love you. I will never stop missing you.

CONTENTS

INTRODUCTION 1

PART 1 | JULIE & JOHN A LOVE STORY 7

Chapter 1 | Hey, You're the One! 9

Chapter 2 | Welcome to The Cancer
Roller Coaster! Buckle Up! 17

Chapter 3 | Hope Springs 31

Chapter 4 | The Beginning of The End 41

Chapter 5 | Saying Goodbye 53

Chapter 6 | What John and His Cancer Taught Me 67

PART 2 | JULIE A REBIRTH STORY 71

Chapter 7 | How Will I Go On? 73

Chapter 8 | Diving Into Grief 79

Chapter 9 | Losing Myself 89

Chapter 10 | Finding Myself 99

Chapter 11 | Moving Forward 105

Chapter12 | Having My Own Back 113

Chapter 13 | Love Wins 117

Part 3 | THE THRIVE PROCESs 121

Chapter 14 | You Too Can Thrive Again 123

Chapter 15 | Trust Yourself 127

Chapter 16 | Honor Your Feelings 133

Chapter 17 | Remain Present   137

Chapter 18 | Invest In Yourself   141

Chapter 19 | Vow to Act   147

Chapter 20 | Embrace the Learning   151

Chapter 21 | #LiveLikeJohnny   157

ACKNOWLEDGEMENTS   161

ABOUT THE AUTHOR   165

INTRODUCTION

If you've picked up this book there are a few things I need to tell you before you actually start the first chapter. I want to start by sharing why I wrote it, why it took me so long to write it, and what I hope you take away from it.

This is a love story. It's written in three parts. Part one is the story of my relationship with my amazing husband John. I'll tell you right up front (spoiler alert) that John dies halfway through the book, at the end of part one. So it's really the story of how our love got us through the most brutal part of our lives together—which ended up being the end of his life. If you're like me, you'll keep hoping against hope that somehow he won't actually die. It's just like every time I watch one of my all-time favorite movies, Apollo 13. They do that routine tank shake and I'm hoping that, by some miracle, there won't be an explosion and Tom Hanks will finally get to walk on the moon. As I worked my way back through the blog from which this book was born in order to mine my story, I found myself in magical thinking, hoping the story had a happy ending even while knowing there was no way it would.

The second part of the story is also a love story. It's the story of finding my way and loving myself through the brutal time after John died. I thought I was prepared for what would happen, since I'd had over a year to get used to the idea of life without him. We hoped for a miracle but were told from the beginning that stage four metastatic melanoma was a terminal cancer. I just never really believed he'd actually die. I honestly don't think he did either. Even before he died, as I shared our story through the blog I wrote (as much for my own processing and sanity as anything else), the seeds for this book were born. Everyone kept saying I should turn it into a book and I agreed. Before John died, my standard answer to that suggestion was that I'd write the book once I had a happy ending. Of course, in my mind, that meant John got his miracle and we lived happily ever after, as we'd planned to do when we married. I honestly could not imagine another ending.

Once he died, I realized I couldn't write the book from where I was because the story wasn't over—in many ways, it had only just begun. I clearly wasn't getting my happy ending and had no idea where I'd go with the book if I did decide to write it. In many ways, I've been writing the story every day these past several years since losing John, redefining my life and figuring out what a future without him would look like.

In March 2017, a year after he died (when I thought I was ready), I hired a book coach—my friend Jim House, "The Book Carver"—flew to San Diego, and fleshed out the bones of this book. I had every intention of completing it before the end of that year. And every time I made a plan to start it, something kept me from taking action. This is very unlike me. I'm an action taker by nature. Sometimes I act on an idea before the plan has even been created. It's made me a great entrepreneur but when it came to writing this book, that drive and focus was nowhere to be found. The October deadline that I'd given myself came and went and I hadn't even started writing.

I now know that a book like this—outlining in great detail the worst time in my life, followed by a complete rebirth of me—can't be written in the middle of the grief brought on by those experiences. And while I realize I'll never stop grieving on some level for all the loss John's death brought, I have finally come to a point where I'm ready to look at that time and what it taught me through a much less painful lens. Don't get me wrong, I'm sure much of this book will absolutely be written through a blur of tears accompanied by a pile of Kleenex on my desk, but I'm finally ready.

So why would I want to put myself through the painful process of writing this book? What's the point? It's about sharing what I've learned and the coping mechanism I inadvertently developed to get through the experience of watching my husband slowly die and then putting my life back together once he was gone. Part three of this book outlines a clear process that came out of this time in my life. I call it the THRIVE process.

Thrive stands for:

Trust yourself
Honor your feelings
Remain present
Invest in yourself
Vow to act
Embrace the learning

The THRIVE process helped me deal with the stress of caretaking for my husband through debilitating cancer treatments and the loss of our life as we knew it. It kept me sane through one emergency after another, nights spent on cots in his hospital room, and the agonizing moment when he took his final breath. It got me out of bed every morning after he died when all I wanted to do was pull the covers over my head and give up. I want to share that process with you through our story together and through my own path alone because I believe it might help you get through any difficult time in your own life.

That's the most important reason. There's also another one. I heard from hundreds of people while I was writing and sharing the blog. They told me that my ability to be raw and honest and to share those very private thoughts and feelings publicly had impacted their lives in a rich and powerful way. That's enough reason for me to want to share the whole story all in one place and with the perspective of the years after the day John died. If you or anyone who reads this book gains even a small appreciation for the gifts in your life because of our story, it's worth it.

Finally, as I wrote this book, it dawned on me that it was more than a story about cancer, death, or even survival through devastating loss. The more I rose above my story to take on the detached narrator role, the more I saw huge similarities between my journey as an entrepreneur, my journey as a caregiving spouse, and then my journey as a grieving widow. There are huge lessons to learn from the roller coaster ride I took with John that I've applied to my journey as an entrepreneur.

What I've learned from this great shift in my life has given me the courage to totally embrace what I love to do, slam the door on things I've done before that made me a great living but didn't "light me up," and trust that whatever I allow to fall away will be replaced with something completely wonderful and perfect for me. And that this will happen even if I can't see a clear definition of what it is or how I'll get there. This has really become the message of this book. Trust where you are right now, embrace everything without labeling it as "good" or "bad," and keep moving forward no matter what.

It works when you're stressed, when you're devastated by loss, when you feel lost and like you don't know who you are (let alone which step to take next), and when you know—in your heart and soul—that you're meant for something different than you're experiencing right now. It gives you the courage to embrace every moment of your current experience and move faithfully, if not confidently, in the direction in which you are being pulled.

I'm excited to share that journey with you. I hope you're excited about taking it with me. We'll go through it together and, if all goes as planned, come out the other side changed in amazing ways we never expected when we started out in Chapter One.

Buckle up and let's do this.

PART 1

JULIE & JOHN

A LOVE STORY

CHAPTER 1

HEY, YOU'RE THE ONE!

"He's a nice guy, but he's not the one." I had just returned from a Match.com blind date and I had called my anxious bestie Sharon with a report, as I always did. In the past several months I'd called her almost weekly with nothing to report. Tonight was no different.

His name was John. We'd met for coffee (my standard Match.com first date) and then walked down to the French restaurant on Main Street for a glass of wine. He was attractive enough, easy to talk to, and very sweet but there was no spark, no chemical attraction for me. I doubted I'd hear from him again but if I did, we'd just remain friends. The hunt for Mr. Right continued.

So I was surprised when that Sunday, as I sat in the movies with my two boys, he texted me from a weekend in Seattle with his kids, checking in and sharing pictures of their adventures. Maybe he was more interested in me than I was in him. Maybe I should reconsider my first, knee-jerk reaction. After all, a strong chemical attraction hadn't really served me all that well through the many men (including two ex-husbands) who had paraded through my life up to that point. Maybe allowing love to grow out of mutual respect was worth a shot.

Since John lived about sixty miles from me, we dated maybe once a week or so for about a month. He would drive over, take me to dinner or a movie, or hang out doing small, honey-do projects around my house. I had a great need for someone with those skills since I was a single mom without them. The more time we spent together, the more time we wanted to spend together. And the more I grew to know him, the more attractive he became.

Yes, he was pretty handsome, but more importantly, he was the most beautiful person on the inside that I've ever met. Positive, kind, funny, and extremely calm and patient. He accepted everyone right where they were and for who they were—me most of all. Before long I began to think that I had quite possibly, after all, indeed found Mr. Right.

I can pinpoint the exact moment I fell in love with John. It was about six weeks into our relationship. We'd had a wonderful, fun evening. He'd given me a tennis lesson and then made me dinner at his place. I spent the night with him for the first time. Sometime, in the middle of the night, as we lay totally absorbed in each other, out of nowhere, he looked me squarely in the eyes and said, "You deserve to be defended." I knew, in that moment, that he was the one who would do that for me for the rest of my life.

He moved in four months later with no fanfare or big pronouncement. We simply decided that we didn't want to live sixty miles apart anymore. He started bringing the few belongings he had home with him from work each night as he drove the forty-five miles back to my house. Space was made in the downstairs closet and boxes were stacked in the garage and before we knew it, my home became our home. It just felt natural and perfectly right.

We lived together for two years, content to share our lives as domestic partners. I'd been married twice and had told him on that first date that I never intended to marry again. I knew he wanted to marry me but, to his credit, he never pushed the issue. There seemed no reason. We were partners in every sense of the word and knew that would never change. Then we took all four of our kids on a weekend camping trip and realized that we made a pretty perfect family. I started to soften to the idea of making it official but still wasn't convinced. It was a random conversation on one of our many road trips a month later that finally changed my mind.

The topic was, "*What would happen if something happened to one of us? If we were in a bad wreck and in the hospital?*" The fact that neither of us would have any authority to make decisions for the other concerned me more than it did him. That had everything to do with the fact that he got along with my family much better than I got along with his. His twin brother Tony, in particular, was not my biggest fan. He didn't like me from the beginning of our relationship and nothing I did ever changed that. I'm guessing it had something to do with the fact that I am a strong, independent, confident woman and I believe I intimidated him. Whatever the reason, I said to John during that conversation, "If anything happened to you, Tony would not only take over, he'd keep me from even seeing you. I have no doubt about that." I don't think John believed that was true but he understood my concern.

We had a Labor Day trip to Las Vegas planned for the following month and it seemed like perfect timing. We planned our wedding in three weeks. If you've never gotten married in Las Vegas, you should. Everyone should. If you're already married, renew your vows. It's an incredible experience and you can get the wedding of your dreams, all inclusive, for about $1500.

We came home happily married in September 2011 and life went on. Kids graduated from high school and went off to college and jobs. My speaking and online training business kept growing, and John quit his municipal job to start his own consulting business—enabling us to have more freedom to travel. We took cruises and road trips. We bought a motorhome and a boat and made amazing memories with family and friends. We remodeled our house. Life was very, very good.

I had found the perfect man for me and we were living the perfect life. I knew, without a shadow of a doubt, that this was the man I would grow old with, happily loving my best friend until the end of my life. He was the one person who completely "got" me, who loved the same sappy TV shows and movies I loved. He was the one person with whom I wanted to share experiences, travel, eat with, sleep with, and love forever. Our love was fun and secure and peaceful. It was my happy place and my sanctuary. He was my home.

He was, indeed, always my defender, always had my back, and always loved me in spite of everything. I believe that most people don't get the chance to be loved that way and I never, ever took it for granted. He was confident enough in his own skin to allow me to be the strong woman that I was. That was a first for me. He also never let me push him around. Once, early in our relationship, we were coming out of Home Depot after a trip to gather odds and ends for some simple home repairs. As he pushed the cart out of the store, I noticed that he wasn't taking the quickest path to my car. I figured he needed a little guidance, so I grabbed the side of the cart to put it on the correct path—that being mine, not his.

He stopped dead in his tracks and forced the cart back to its original trajectory. He looked at me and asked, "Are you steering my cart?"

"Well, yeah," I replied, "You're going the wrong way. We're parked over there and this way is faster."

"I know exactly where we're parked," he said. Then gently but firmly, "Don't do that. Don't steer my cart." There was no drama, no blaming or making me feel like a controlling bitch, just him letting me know that it wasn't ok to push him around. We used that analogy throughout the rest of our lives together. I'd get a little pushy or controlling and he'd say, "Stop steering my cart." Then we'd both smile and I'd get the not-so-subtle hint and back off.

In the middle of October 2013, as I was getting dressed for the day, John came into our bedroom with a concerned look on his face. "Feel that," he said, rubbing his leg next to his left groin. Obliging, I felt a small, hard lump, about the size of a golf ball. "How long has that been there?" I asked, a little alarmed. "About 2 weeks," he replied. Exasperated, I admonished him. "You need to get that checked."

Two weeks later, after an ultrasound that led to a surgical biopsy, I sat in the day surgery waiting room with John's twin brother and daughter and waited for what I had to believe were routine results. His surgeon came out looking somber and called us into what I came to call "the bad news room." The first words out of his mouth were "I'm so sorry."

John had cancer. It felt surreal, like I'd somehow jumped momentarily into someone else's life or come into a theatre in the middle of a movie. There's no way my healthy, happy, never-sick husband had cancer. It just wouldn't sink in.

And not just any cancer. Four days later we received a call from the surgeon who had the full and final results of the biopsy. Melanoma. He had said the day of the biopsy that he hoped it wasn't melanoma, because melanoma was badass and angry and one of the most aggressive forms of cancer. I freaked a little and John took it completely in stride. His default from that day forward was to go into problem solver mode and look at what our nexts steps were. He refused to ever give in. As long as he had another weapon at his disposal, he would pick it up and fight.

CHAPTER 2

WELCOME TO THE CANCER ROLLER COASTER! BUCKLE UP!

Action has always been the key word in my life. I tend to move through life at a pretty good pace. I'm a planner and I'm super organized—the more information I have, the better I like it.

What I rapidly learned as we started our journey through John's cancer diagnosis and treatment was that, to cancer, my need to take action, have a plan, or be in any sort of control was just a huge joke. Cancer just laughed at me every day. The sign in the cancer waiting room says, "Please have a seat." It should add, "You'll be here for a while." When I'd go up to the front desk to ask what was going on or what was happening next, cancer handed me a magazine and invited me to sit back down... and wait.

Waiting is a key component of any cancer journey. Wait for tests to be scheduled, and then wait for the results of tests that could change the course of your life. Wait for an appointment with a specialist. Wait to get into a clinical trial that could save your life. It felt like being suspended in mid-air, straining my toes toward the ground to attempt to regain my footing but not quite being able to reach. Of course, our goal while we waited was to always stay focused on the outcome we wanted. Most of the time, we could do that.

But, no matter how vigilant I was, it was inevitable that the "what ifs" would start creeping in now and then. In those moments especially, I wanted to JUST DO something, to take action, make a plan, know EXACTLY what was next. But cancer was running the show and I wasn't. I can't say I ever got good at waiting but I definitely got better at it. I really had no choice.

The weeks after John's diagnosis were filled with waiting, choices, and then action. Once we'd met with a local oncologist and been referred to the larger Seattle Cancer Care Alliance (about 350 miles west of us), he was scheduled for a radical lymphadenectomy and thirty-three lymph nodes were removed from the area where the original lump had been found. At the time, this was the only treatment available for metastatic melanoma. There was no chemotherapy or radiation for this type of cancer. So we hung a lot of hope on this procedure. On Christmas eve of 2013—two weeks after the surgery—we got the news that none of the lymph nodes they had removed contained any cancer. He was, in effect, cancer free. It was a true Christmas miracle, the kind that happens in sappy movies with happy endings. We had dodged a bullet, we thought. The cancer hadn't spread and we could chalk it up to a blip on the radar of our otherwise happy life and move on (if more cautiously and with periodic checkups to ensure he was still cancer free).

We went back to our lives. John was healthy and sailed through his three-month checkup in March 2014 with flying, cancer-free colors. We began remodeling our house and making plans for a fun, busy summer.

Then he noticed a lump in the area where he'd had the surgery. The exact same area where he'd found the first lump. I had a surreal déjà vu moment one morning in our bedroom when I noticed he looked distracted and concerned. Our eyes met and he asked me for the second time in just over six months, "Feel that," and pointed to his left groin. Again, I asked him how long the lump had been there. "A few days," he said. He told me that at first he thought maybe it was scar tissue but now was getting concerned because scar tissue doesn't grow perceptibly every day. This time I didn't have to tell him he needed to get it checked.

After a visit to his GP who sent him straight to the hospital for a CT scan, John was referred back to his melanoma oncologist,

Dr. John Thompson at Seattle Cancer Care Alliance. We had to wait a tortuous week for that appointment. Dr. Thompson was alarmed at the rate of growth of the lump and did a needle biopsy. After nearly another week, we got the call we'd been dreading.

I had just come in from running errands and John was sitting at the kitchen table on the phone. He saw me and said, "Hold on Dr. Thompson. Let me put you on speaker." Our eyes met and I sat down next to him at the table. John put the phone down between us and took my hand as we listened to Dr. Thompson. "I'm afraid it's not good news," he started.

The biopsy had come back positive for melanoma, indicating that the cancer was back and spreading. There were also several other spots on the CT scan in his abdominal and renal area that were now assumed to be cancer as well. Worst of all, his diagnosis was changed from stage three to stage four melanoma. We learned that day that the survivability rate for this type of cancer is less than 10% over five years. There was also no FDA-approved treatment beyond the radical lymphadenectomy that John had already had. His only hope was to get into a clinical trial with experimental immunotherapy drugs. With more apologies and the promise to let us know about a spot in a trial, Dr. Thompson hung up. I sat stunned, tearing up, and looked at John. He was a rock. He smiled at me and said, "It's ok. This is new information and now we go from here." He wasn't outwardly upset. He held me and I had a good cry, and then he got up and went back to work as if nothing had happened.

A few days later, John came home from work and called a family meeting with my two boys and me in the living room. He was more serious than usual, but that wasn't unexpected considering the fact that we were still reeling from the conversation with Dr. Thompson. He got straight to the point.

"I talked to my oncologist this morning and asked the million dollar question… how long do I have? He told me that if I do nothing, odds are about a year."

My heart stopped and I took slow, deep breaths, determined not to break down in front of my kids. "I just want you to know, I don't plan to do nothing," John said. "We're going to do whatever we can to beat those odds." I told him that I hadn't signed up for just one more year when I married him and that I wouldn't settle for less than thirty more, so if he came to me at eighty and said he had twelve months to live, so be it. But not now.

We made a plan and went to war. We agreed that we were willing to put anything "natural" into his body that wouldn't hurt him if we felt that it could help him. That included essential oils, juice from the most fresh, organic greens we could find, and medical grade cannabis oil therapy. There were a few clinical trials available to him that increased his chances of survival to about 20% and we aggressively pursued them. A few weeks later, a spot miraculously opened up in the most promising trial available and John was the perfect candidate.

His doctor did not tell us this trial would cure him. In fact, he made a point of making sure we understood that nothing could do that. Our objective was to continue doing everything humanly possible to slow down the spread and growth so he'd still be around when science did make a significant medical discovery that could cure him. Our life became about living with cancer indefinitely, hoping something we were doing would create a miracle.

John's mom always said that he wouldn't say shit if he had a mouthful. It was honestly one of the things I loved most about him. He was an eternal optimist at heart and rarely ever complained. Even through his diagnosis and the twists and turns our lives took after that day, he mostly remained his grounded, happy, non-complaining self.

Over the course of the following year, John was put through the ringer. The immunotherapy clinical trial initially worked to shrink his tumors and then almost killed him with crippling side effects that caused ongoing issues with his kidneys and pancreas. As his doctor said to us one day, "This is the Puritan approach to cancer treatment. The more you suffer, the greater the results." He had multiple infections that required daily antibiotics, fluids, or blood infusions, and many hospitalizations. We also spent a lot of time at The University of Washington Medical Center as John endured numerous surgeries to deal with the aggressive tumors that refused to be affected by anything we did to stop them.

The tumor in his groin was particularly aggressive and, by the time he had the second surgery to remove it, it had grown to over seventeen centimeters—about the size of a baseball. We used radiation to shrink it initially, but all that did was weaken the already-thin skin covering the tumor and cause it to open up, exposing him to a raging infection which he endured for over a month before they finally agreed to remove the tumor. That surgery required a plastic surgeon to remove a huge flap of skin from his outer thigh to cover the gaping hole left behind by the tumor. We spent over a week in the hospital for the surgery in July 2015. By February 2016 when he died, the tumor was back and larger than it had been before the previous surgery.

In the process, I watched John age before my eyes. His hair went almost completely white in the span of less than a month and he lost much of his stamina. This was a man who normally went ninety miles an hour from the moment his feet hit the floor early in the morning until he dropped into bed late at night. So the day I came home from running errands to find him napping in the middle of a busy day (when I knew he had one hundred other things to get done) brought home to me how much the treatment was taking out of him.

I vividly remember a moment when he was at his most ill during the first trial. He seemed to disappear. He was just not there, as he went inside himself to do what he needed to do to deal with the physical fallout of poisoning his body. At his lowest point, I looked into his eyes and pleaded, "Just promise me you're still in there." He smiled weakly at me and just nodded. It was heartbreaking and frightening.

Throughout the two and a half year journey of John's cancer treatment, our predominant mindset was that if the treatment was killing the cancer, the side effects were worth it. It reminded me of a conversation I'd had with my brother Mark in the middle of his radiation treatment for stage four throat cancer a few years prior to John's cancer (which he survived—he's still cancer free as of today). I asked him how he could keep going through the horrific side effects of the head and neck radiation he was getting and he said simply, "This is the treatment for throat cancer and the alternative is sort of final."

The one thing John never lost was his sense of humor. He refused to focus on the negative and looked for the good in every single day. Our lives had changed dramatically in just a short few months but our relationship deepened, as did my love and appreciation for him. My husband was brave, positive, happy, and patient. These qualities served him, and all those around him, well throughout his cancer journey.

As for me, I lost myself for quite a while as well, as I held on by a thread and took it one day (sometimes one minute) at a time. I cared for him and dealt with all of the things that went along with his cancer while still doing my best to maintain my "regular" life. I also came to realize just how much we lived in partnership in our day-to-day lives and how much he did for me and us—from laundry to dishes, to making the bed and lots of other little things in between. When those all fell on my shoulders, it was a bigger adjustment than I even realized at the time.

When I wasn't dealing with John's treatment schedule, insurance claims, or the side effects from the clinical trials, I was head down, working, doing my best to keep my business afloat to support us financially. Someone told me when John was diagnosed that being the caregiver of a cancer patient is like a full-time job. I didn't really believe it at the time. Trust me, it's true. Only the other full-time jobs in your life, like your ACTUAL job or your kids or your aging parents, don't go away. It impacted every part of my life and the lives of my kids and those closest to me. It's an unseen but very real side effect of cancer.

In fact, cancer comes into your life like an uninvited guest. It takes up residence, stealing the master suite for its own, whether you like it or not. An extremely needy and impolite guest, it invades your space, your thoughts, your time, and your daily existence. It decides how your day, your week, or your month goes. It demands that you change your plans at the drop of a hat and decides whether or not you work that day.

It doesn't care if your kids are sick, your parents need your support, or your boss or client is expecting you to finish a job by a deadline. It's selfish and it doesn't care. Worst of all, you can't circle a date on the calendar, looking forward to it's departure. It may never leave.

It removes your core stability, making the ground beneath your feet that was once solid and firm, movable and unstable. "Just see if you can get your footing," it taunts. Feeling a little too comfortable with your life? Settling into a new "normal?" No worries. Cancer takes care of that for you. You better learn to dance through the chaos, because there's gonna be chaos. In the blink of an eye, things will change again, you'll have to adapt to a new set of challenges, your life will turn.

Surviving an uninvited guest requires a sense of humor. And diligence, as you pay attention to the rare times when the guest is out or sleeping and you can reclaim your space for a little while. This new, constant presence that may never go away requires every coping tool you've ever learned. And some days, I found that just making it through the day as I navigated around this uninvited guest was the best I could hope for.

I turned into a helicopter wife—especially after the frightening week in the hospital during the first clinical trial when his kidneys began to shut down and he almost died—constantly looking for any symptoms or signs of a return to that nightmare. I know my hovering drove him a little crazy, especially during the times when he felt pretty good, but he put up with it. He understood and was really patient with me.

This was also completely new emotional territory for me. I'd never been through anything like it and I couldn't seem to get a handle on how to be a person who seemed to have lost her drive and ambition, and who succumbed to uncontrollable waves of sadness multiple times throughout the day. Actually, it wasn't just sadness. It was fear at the deepest level and on so many levels, and frustration that my default positive attitude seemed to have gone on an extended vacation with no expected return date.

This state in which I found myself would return multiple times over the course of the next two and a half years as we fought this battle together. I felt helpless and tired, pissed off one minute and terrified and devastated the next, generally fighting to stay in the moment and not just lose it pretty much every minute.

At the end of the day, as the incredibly resilient Lena Horne once said, "It's not the load that breaks you down, it's the way you carry it." Being the one who loves someone with cancer may be harder than having it yourself. I can't say for sure because I've never been diagnosed, but I've loved three very important people in my life through it and it sucks. It's scary and hard and all-encompassing. Most days while John was sick, what I really wanted to do the minute I woke up to the reality that the beautiful, perfect-for-me man lying next to me in bed had terminal cancer, was pull the sheets up over my head and go back to sleep so it all just went away. The reality of my life was that lots of people relied on me and I couldn't afford to give in (or give up).

So I chose to carry what felt like a very heavy load, with gratitude and grace and as much strength as I could draw from all of the incredible blessings in my life. It was a daily choice and some days came more easily than others. I began to develop a pattern for surviving this emotional firestorm that was our new life. The first part of that is the first step in the THRIVE process... trusting myself. I learned to really listen to my intuition. More than once, I allowed that still-small voice inside me to guide me, trusting that it knew better than I did what was best for me and for us.

I didn't fight my feelings but honored them (the second step in the THRIVE process), allowing them to come and just being present with them when they did. Once I'd worked through those first two steps in my process, I inevitably began to look at what I could control—forcing myself to stay present with what was happening and this moved me from victim to proactive participant (the third step in the process). I formulated a plan, got invested in following it through (step number four), and took action based on what I knew (step number five). Then, once the current crisis had been navigated, I'd take to the blog and write about it, always forcing myself to look for the learning in every situation (the final step). I didn't always go through the process in this order, but generally this was how it played out. And while I didn't realize it at the time, that process became my survival mechanism. It evolved into the THRIVE process I still use today.

> **T**rust yourself
> **H**onor your feelings
> **R**emain present
> **I**nvest in a plan
> **V**ow to act
> **E**mbrace the learning

During part three of this book, we'll delve more deeply into each part of the THRIVE process and I'll show you how to use it in your own life.

CHAPTER 3

HOPE SPRINGS

So often, our cancer journey was about moving from crisis to crisis, adjusting to one new development after another, and focusing on the issue at hand. The stress that accompanied that was unique and challenging, for sure.

What I came to understand was that those times when we weren't necessarily facing an emergency—but instead proactively figuring out what came next, researching options, getting appointments scheduled with the proper doctors, and waiting (always waiting)—created a more intense, difficult type of stress. It was harder to see or understand because it crept up on us, but I found it much more challenging in the long run to deal with.

In early March 2015, we met with Dr. Thompson for John's "routine" monthly checkup. It was clear to us that we had reached the place in John's cancer progression where the doctors weren't telling him what to do anymore, but giving him options and leaving the choices up to him. It reminded me of when Monty Hall on the game show *Let's Make A Deal* used to ask contestants *"Will it be door #1, door #2, or door #3?"* Sitting at home in the living room, I remember yelling my (always correct) choice at the TV (not that the ridiculous people dressed up like hippos or aliens ever listened).

For John, there were also three doors. Door #1 was to keep walking down the road we'd been on and hope that the quality of life John had left, for as long as he had left, was as positive and healthy as possible. No one was willing to speculate on (because no one really knew) how long that road might be.

What was behind door #2 was a new immunotherapy miracle drug called Keytruda. It had the potential to cure John's cancer if it didn't completely annihilate his pancreas and colon first. Worst case scenario, according to his doctor, his pancreas would completely dissolve (and he wouldn't survive that). Best case scenario, we wiped out the cancer and he had several more years (if not a whole lifetime) of life. But—and this was a big but—his quality of life while he was on that drug could be really, really bad because there was no doubt that he would have issues with his pancreas, which at that point was already unhappy. Dr. Thompson advised against door #2. John's local oncologist (who, by his own admission was NOT a melanoma specialist) clearly thought he should go for it based on three of his own melanoma patients who had experienced "miraculous" results.

Behind door #3 was a clinical trial at The National Cancer Institute (NCI) in Bethesda, Maryland. This was an intense stem cell treatment (called TIL for tumor infiltrating lymphocytes) that would require several months of upheaval in our lives and could kill him. If he was accepted, there would be a surgery to remove white blood cells from one of his tumors, a three- to six-week break for them to grow billions of new cells from those they extracted, and then a second trip to Maryland for him to undergo aggressive chemotherapy in the intensive care unit of the hospital to wipe out his entire immune system (and all of his current white blood cells). Then he'd receive the new T-cells and we'd pray this treatment worked. It had a 50% success rate (just like everything else he'd been offered).

Monty, Monty, Monty… Which door should we choose?

It felt like an overwhelming choice for me. As I've said, I'm a planner and I like order. I like to know what's happening, when it's happening, and what I need to do to show up prepared. While I'd gotten better at rolling with the cancer punches in the year and a half since John's diagnosis, it was still not something that came at all naturally for me. Up until that point, at least we'd had an idea about what came next. Someone was telling us which door to choose. Now it was up to us. We talked it through together, but in the end it was

John's decision. It was his life. Whatever he decided, I'd be on board.

Not only did we need to decide what to do, but we needed to do it quickly. Until we settled on a course of action, John wasn't getting any treatment. He had to be off of every other medication or treatment in order to be eligible for the NCI program. Since he had the BRAF gene mutation that accelerated the growth of his tumors, we literally watched things progress almost daily.

After quite a bit of conversation and weighing the pros and cons, we decided that the NCI trial was his best bet. The application process for that program required a lot of coordinating with John's current doctors and getting records and tests sent to NCI as soon as possible. There were lots of boxes that needed to be ticked in order for him to even schedule his first assessment appointment. Once we decided on this course of action, it seemed as though it took forever to get everything together. We were stuck in a holding pattern, waiting on doctors and labs and hospital administrators for information we needed in order to complete the application process.

I just wanted to scream a lot of the time. I felt like Shirley MacLaine in that hospital scene in *Terms of Endearment* where it's time for her daughter's pain meds and nobody's doing anything. I wanted to scream "DO SOMETHING!"

Part of me understood that he was obviously not the only cancer patient being treated by his doctors and that they were probably moving as fast as they could. Not to sound selfish, but he was the only one of their cancer patients I cared about. He was my biggest priority and I'd do anything to move things along for him. And the waiting was hell.

Worst of all was the unknown in our lives. We couldn't make plans, even for the current week, let alone the following month. We had to be ready to move at the drop of a hat in case he was able to get in to see the appropriate doctor. We lived in a constant state of "hurry up and wait."

In mid-August, we got the call that NCI was willing to assess John to see if he would be a good fit for their trial. We flew back to Bethesda, Maryland and spent a long, grueling day on assessment tests and intake appointments. At the end of the day things looked good. John was a strong candidate, generally healthy and a good fit for all of their criteria. The only roadblock was the most recent CT scan he'd had that showed three large, aggressive tumors in his intestines. Since the treatment was so aggressive, the presence of these tumors could kill him. If the tumors couldn't be removed, he wouldn't be a candidate.

We flew home with high hopes and began to research our next steps for clearing the tumors from John's intestines. He had a colonoscopy and we scheduled an appointment with an oncology gastroenterologist at Seattle Cancer Care Alliance to explore our options for having the tumors removed so he could start the trial. While we waited for that appointment, John's health and daily quality of life began to go downhill.

He was running a constant fever, had no energy, and said that everything tasted bad so virtually stopped eating unless he had to.

For me, it was agony watching his health decline so rapidly and not be able to do anything about it. I could go from complete devastation to intense fear to total fury and frustration at the lack of options open to us, all in a single short hour. My emotions were all over the place. In my worst moments, I just wanted off this ride. I didn't want to do this anymore.

I wanted to go back to the way our life was not quite two years before, before we knew anything about melanoma or clinical trials or side effects. I wanted my healthy husband back. I wanted to make plans and keep them. I wanted to jump out of bed excited about the day instead of dreading what might come next.

On better days I remembered what a strong man I was married to, how he accepted every single shift—good or bad—with grace and humor. I remembered how much he loved me and how much I loved him and how lucky we were to have each other. I focused on the things in my life for which I was grateful and on the fact that, if I had to go through this, I wouldn't have wanted to do it with anyone but John.

On October 6th, 2015, we finally saw the oncology gastroenterologist. He pulled up John's most recent CT scan for us to see. The news was not good. He pointed out that there were many more tumors than we had originally thought and there was no way to tell which one was causing the bleeding we'd been dealing with for months.

As he identified tumor after tumor on the scan, pointing to each with the tip of his pen, the reality of what we were facing sunk in. Surgery wasn't an option. Even if they could identify and remove all of the tumors, the doctor told us, he wouldn't survive the surgery because of how spread out the tumors were. They would essentially have to remove over half of his small intestine, which wasn't an option. That meant the NIH study, his last real chance at treatment, was no longer an option either.

I looked at the doctor and said, "So what's our next move?" Without missing a beat he replied, "You don't have any more options." Then, looking at John he said, "Go home and get your affairs in order. You're looking at a few months at most." And then he shook our hands and walked out of the room.

The five-hour drive back to Walla Walla was difficult as we began facing this new reality. We talked about how he wanted to die, what would happen to me once he was gone, and how to best prepare our kids. He reiterated, as he'd said many times in the past few months, how he was ok with dying, how grateful he was for the life he'd lived and how proud of his kids he was. He also told me what he thought would happen after he died.

John was always what I called a "quiet Christian." He had a deep and abiding Christian faith but kept it to himself. His "personal relationship with Jesus" was truly personal. He said he believed our relationship would continue after he was gone, that he wouldn't be missing anything. He believed he'd experience every milestone, birth, death, and event in our lives, just from another dimension. He said he didn't know if it would happen in real time for him as it happened to us or if he'd experience it all at once in the moment that he passed, but he truly believed that he would experience it. "It will just be like I'm in the next room. That's how you have to think about it. Like I'm here but just not in the same room with you."

A few weeks later John had his first CT scan since August. We did it because he was going to need a feeding tube in the near future and they had to be sure that there were no tumors in his stomach that would create problems with that. Even though we were pretty sure what we'd see when we looked at the scans side-by-side with his doctor, we were still secretly hoping there would be some miraculous shrinkage of the tumors. I fantasized about his doctor rubbing his head in confusion and disbelief saying, "It's the darndest thing and we can't explain it, but the tumors are just gone!" A girl can dream.

The results were devastating for me. The tumors had grown significantly. The one on his Pancreas had almost doubled in size and was more involved in the organ. I was also watching the toll the cancer was taking on his body. He had lost over thirty pounds and tired easily. Some days it was a struggle to eat and he was not able to keep down what he did manage to take in. We were having issues keeping his blood pressure up and he struggled to stay hydrated, so daily IV drips to keep up his fluids were becoming commonplace. He also began having weekly blood transfusions because of the slow internal bleeding caused by the tumors. His joints ached and he struggled with edema in his lower legs and ankles.

I also watched the toll his cancer took on my body. The stress hormone was more powerful than I ever imagined. I gained the thirty pounds he lost, had pretty much a perpetual menstrual cycle for the entire last year of his cancer, struggled to sleep, and had dark circles and serious bags under my eyes. All of my adult life I've looked younger than my age but now, I felt like I'd aged ten years, virtually overnight. I almost didn't recognize the woman in the mirror looking back at me every morning. It was a challenge to relax and I was constantly monitoring his state, asking if he was ok, and doing my best not to worry. I worked at home every day but was often distracted by his needs, so that drive and determination I always relied on as an entrepreneur felt more like a curse than a blessing.

Over the next ten days we met with a social worker from the hospital to talk about palliative care versus hospice and we had the difficult conversation with his local oncologist about how we would know when it was time for hospice. At this point we were still not giving up. The problem was, the only thing really left for us was a miracle. Melanoma is such a tricky, aggressive cancer that there just aren't that many options once you get to the point at which we currently found ourselves.

I cried buckets of tears during these weeks of transition and preparation. The pain was physical and intense and came over me like waves, when I least expected it, at the most unexpected times. I could literally feel my heart breaking. I truly believe that my grieving journey began on that October day. I grieved the things he would miss unless we got our miracle. I thought about our kids and how this would impact them.

I thought about the life we had planned and all of the things we were ready to start doing once we became "empty nesters" the following year when our youngest, Eli, graduated from high school, and about how I would manage if I had to do those things alone. I thought about how perfectly John loved me, how perfect he was for me, and I couldn't imagine my life without that love.

Mostly, I thought about how much my life had changed because of him. How I moved through the world differently because of the way he had loved me. How much I loved his kids and the gift he gave me of the daughter I never thought I'd have. How the previous six years we'd had together had been the best of my life.

I also realized that, no matter how much longer we had together, those years had changed me for good and that I would not trade them—even to avoid the pain I was currently experiencing—for anything.

CHAPTER 4

THE BEGINNING
OF THE END

As human beings, we measure our lives in milestones. When you're terminally ill (or you love someone who is), every day becomes a milestone. Because of that, the bigger milestones, the ones healthy people count, like holidays, anniversaries, and birthdays take on even more significance. You begin to count those milestones, to look forward to them, to hope for them. And always lingering in the back of your mind is the question, "Will this be the last?"

As Thanksgiving 2015 approached, John was doing alright. He couldn't work or do anything very physical but he wasn't feeling as horrible as he had been the previous month. He came to me one day and said, "I want to have one last adventure."

He loved road trips so we packed up our thirty-two foot motorhome with my boys, my mom, and our two dogs and headed south to San Jose, California where John's two kids were living. He wanted to celebrate as a family and he wanted to get in that motorhome and drive again, to feel like his old self—in charge and at the wheel. The main reason I agreed was because I knew that, by traveling in the motorhome, if he did start to feel bad, he could lay down on the bed and let me drive.

He was able to drive the 4 hours from our home in Walla Walla to Portland but by the time we arrived that night, he was exhausted and struggling to keep warm. Getting (and staying) warm became a constant problem for him from this point on and by the last month of his life, it was virtually impossible to get him warmed up. He never complained but I could see how sick he felt that night and by the next morning, things hadn't improved much. He started out behind the wheel but after we stopped for lunch I suggested he lay down and let me drive and he didn't argue with me. For most of the rest of the trip, he slept and my son Sam and I drove. I was afraid he wasn't going to be able to enjoy our trip at all but he surprised us all and, after a good night's sleep once we arrived in San Jose, he rallied.

On Thanksgiving day I posted on Facebook, "We are blessed by so much and are choosing to focus on the gratitude we feel for today without thinking too much about tomorrow. Among the blessings we're counting is another day together spent with those we hold most dear. As you celebrate Thanksgiving with whomever you love this year, remember to mark that milestone, to treasure it, to hold on to it, and to understand how important it is in the scope of your life, however long that may be."

We had a wonderful few days as a family, spending time together, touring the Google campus where our son-in-law worked, going out to eat, and laughing a lot. It was exactly what we'd hoped it would be and I know it meant the world to John. It was clear to all of us that this would be his last Thanksgiving and the fact that we'd been able to spend it all together making such special memories was a huge gift.

The best part of that trip for John was the drive home, since he actually felt really good and was able to drive the entire way. In retrospect I realize that it was probably the last time in his life that he felt like he was in control. He knew he was dying but during those few days of driving home, he could forget about that and enjoy something that he loved to do.

Once we got home things began to move rapidly. We started making difficult decisions about what would happen after he died and finalizing the details for things like his headstone and memorial service. John was determined to get these things completely figured out so that I wouldn't have to deal with them once he was gone. He reiterated more than once that he'd had a great life, had no regrets, and was ready for whatever came next. He also began working on a few small physical legacies to leave his kids and wanted to put together a slideshow for his service so that was done as well. It was a very odd thing, he said, to be in the position to be able to make these plans while he was still living.

Through it all, this amazing man remained cheerful, grateful, and positive. He got up every day, showered, shaved, and got dressed. Most days he was on the couch asleep by noon—but when he felt good, he still worked a little or "tinkered" with stuff in the garage. He did it because it made him happy, but also because it was important to him that I feel supported. His love for me was always totally supportive, and making sure I knew how much he loved me was a top priority for him.

When you are properly loved by the one who was meant for you all along, you wear that knowledge like a warm coat when you venture out into the world. It makes you who you are and keeps you connected to home. It makes any place you are with the one that you love, your home. I traveled a lot in the six and a half years John and I were together, for work and for fun. Once I found him, I never felt alone when I was on the road. I always knew he was there at home, loving me steadily and completely and supporting me, no matter what I was up to.

It changed the way I moved through the world. It gave me confidence and an ease that I lacked before I met him. He was this amazing person in the world who loved me completely no matter what and who had my back in any situation. Knowing that gave me wings and grounded me, all at the same time.

The one sentence I heard more than any other in those last few months was, "I can't imagine what you're going through."

As I watched John get weaker and thinner and fight to make it through each day and night while his cancer worked to steal every ounce of energy he had, I had to agree. I couldn't imagine it either.

I couldn't have imagined the love I had with him. I thought I had dreamed of it, but it had been oh so much better than I had ever imagined. I couldn't have imagined anyone I loved so much, and had searched for, for so long, being diagnosed with terminal cancer. That was something that happened to other people. They had my compassion and sympathy but never, in my wildest dreams, would I have thought it would happen to us.

I certainly couldn't have imagined accepting the reality that I was watching my sweet love die.

And honestly, I couldn't imagine the day I would actually lose him. Even though I knew it was coming soon, I couldn't wrap my mind around it. He was so intertwined in my life that I couldn't fathom doing absolutely anything without him. He was the one I laughed with, loved with, consulted and processed with, confided in, and loved to spend time with. He was my best friend, my lover, and the love of my life. I couldn't imagine losing him.

Once he died, I knew I'd be walking through the world alone. If I was traveling, he wouldn't be there to call at the end of the day to share my adventures. I did hope that I would still feel that connection to him, that that warm coat of love that

I'd worn every day since the day I fell in love with him would still connect me to him. That he'd still somehow be able to give me the answers I needed when I needed them. He believed he would.

In mid-December, John was hospitalized for the final time, ostensibly to remove another large tumor that had formed above the original tumor site on his upper groin and, more importantly, to attempt to get a feeding tube inserted. It wasn't a planned hospitalization but we weren't getting the support we needed in Walla Walla. We felt he needed a feeding tube and had been told by his general surgeon that, at the end of his life, given the many tumors in his intestines, a feeding tube would improve his quality (and possibly even quantity) of life significantly.

When we asked his gastroenterologist in Walla Walla to perform the operation his response was, "What would be the point? He's only got a few months at most to live." Perhaps anticipating this response, his general surgeon had also told us that if we couldn't get the surgery done in Walla Walla, he recommended that we go to the University of Washington Medical Center in Seattle and have it done there. We'd been waiting over two weeks to get someone in Seattle to get back to us about it and weren't having any luck.

One afternoon, after watching him struggle with fevers from the increasingly infected tumor for several days, my "had enough" meter (as John would say) just broke and I made a decision. "Pack a bag. We're going to Seattle today," I told him. It was a Sunday and we didn't have an appointment but we drove straight to the emergency room. Here's what I discovered that night… when you show up with stage four metastatic cancer AND have a history of MRSA (a nasty, virtually impossible-to-cure form of the Staphylococcus virus that John had gotten years before from a previous infection), you get a room in a big hurry. I was counting on that. Within an hour, John had been admitted and scheduled for surgery to remove the tumor the next morning. When we met with his surgeon, I asked about the feeding tube, and he said he'd have the gastroenterologist come consult with us.

Within a day, he'd been scheduled for the tube placement the following day. I remember talking with the doctor after the surgery, after he'd told me the tube was in place and all had gone well. "Could you see the tumor on his Duodenum?" I asked. "Oh yes. That's a very large, very angry tumor," he said. I asked if it would be possible to remove it and he said not only no, but that even if they could manage to remove it and John survived, it would be back within a few months. It was finally this tumor that killed him, growing so large that it completely blocked off his stomach. In the end, he starved to death.

This was one of the many times I was grateful for my strong (some call it forceful) personality, and for my ability to employ step number one of the THRIVE process. I listened to my intuition and I trusted myself. If I had not advocated, even pushed, for that feeding tube, the end of John's life would have been much worse. The feeding tube is meant to provide nutrition. For the last six weeks or so of his life—before he went on to hospice—it was literally the only nutrition he was getting, but what our surgeon had told us was that it goes both ways and can also be used to extract liquid from the stomach to prevent vomiting.

We were told toward the end of his life that the feeding tube probably gave him two to three extra weeks. Those are weeks I will cherish forever. If I ever come face-to-face with the gastroenterologist from Walla Walla who refused to do the surgery, I will definitely have some choice words for him. How dare he deprive us of any time with my husband. Who was he to make that decision?

We left the hospital that Friday, loaded down with several boxes of nutritional feeding solution, supplies, and detailed instructions. It was my intention to head home but John insisted that we drive south to Portland for my annual family Christmas party at my sister's home. He knew this would be his last chance to celebrate with them and didn't want to miss it. It was a challenging three-hour drive. John was sick the entire way and no matter how much heat I turned on, he was chilled and shivering in between bouts of vomiting.

About twenty minutes from my sister's house, he looked at me, stricken, and said, "My wedding ring is gone." He'd grown so thin that it had fallen off somewhere between his hospital room and the car. I was devastated. We called the hospital but no one had found it. When we arrived at my sister's, I got John situated under some blankets inside the house and searched the car but to no avail. It seemed the ring was gone.

After everything we'd been through in the past few months, this singular, seemingly insignificant event totally devastated me. It just felt like such a huge symbol (or maybe omen). Before every surgery over the past two years, John would hand me his ring just before heading down the hall and say, "See you in five minutes," with a wink. It was huge and I'd put it on my thumb and anchor it with my own thumb ring. It became my "worry stone" during those long waiting room hours. So that night, as I unpacked one of the bags of supplies and found it, my heart leapt with joy. We immediately wrapped surgical tape around it so it wouldn't fall off again.

Adjusting to the feeding tube was a much bigger challenge than we had anticipated. Starting in the summer of 2015, about six months before he died, John just couldn't bring himself to eat. I found out later that cancer makes everything taste bad so it made sense. Once he got the tube, we had to work our way up to 1000 calories a day but it didn't always work out. Sometimes he would throw up the hard-earned nutrition. Those were the worst days. He'd lost a lot of weight and was down to a skeletal—for his 6'2" frame—154 pounds by late December. Christmas was stressful, with family visits and the usual traditions feeling more like chores than joyful occasions for me.

We were both struggling. He was physically and mentally exhausted and had no reserve. Simple tasks like taking a shower or walking up the stairs completely wore him out. His always-present smile had been absent for several weeks and it was becoming harder and harder to help him find it. While at my sister's for the holiday party, I had thrown my back out and had been dealing with muscle spasms that left me incapacitated for a few days and required an emergency room visit and steroid injections. I was barely holding on emotionally. There was nothing I could do to ease his discomfort—when he had one of his horrible chills, or experienced multiple night sweats—and that helpless feeling was extremely challenging for me. I was usually able to maintain a fairly even emotional keel throughout the day, but I went to bed every night feeling overwhelmed with grief and worry, and cried in his arms. He would hold me, feeling helpless himself and apologizing because he knew there was nothing he could say or do that would make it better.

At this point, my primary job had become to take care of John but it felt to him like I was being bossy and telling him what to do all the time, which annoyed him. Add the fact that both of us were exhausted, and too often our interactions began to feel contentious. I hated that and did my best to never take things personally, but our relationship was changing. I was now more his caregiver than his wife. It was a role I gladly embraced but it was a devastating realization nonetheless.

When someone dies from a terminal illness, they gradually fade away. It's the most heartbreaking thing I've ever been through. Some days I would stand at the window and stare out of it, seeing if I could imagine what it would feel like, what my life would be like, once he was gone. It was probably a bit of a morbid thing to do, but someone told me if I could imagine what was coming, it would make it easier to take.

I could not imagine how my life would possibly go on once he was gone. It was beyond the scope of what I could cope with at that point. I walked around with a lump in my throat, doing everything I could not to lose it in any given moment. It was the end of the year and everywhere I looked, blog posts and magazine articles encouraged me to plan for the upcoming new year. All they actually did was make me feel numb. How could I plan for something I had no idea how to handle?

Every day it felt like my life was a test that I was failing.

Again, the THRIVE process was my lifeline. I used it to stay present with my own feelings, allow myself to feel whatever came up, take inspired action based on tuning into my feelings, and to continue writing our story through the blog—looking for the learning as I processed all that was happening through my writing. The THRIVE process helped me navigate the most difficult time in my life with some semblance of control and I believe, in many ways, it kept me sane. I still actively use it today.

CHAPTER 5

SAYING GOODBYE

Cancer steals more than just the life it threatens. It steals the life that could have been. It steals the hopes and dreams and plans that have been made. And, if you're not careful, it steals what joy is left in life.

For the final three months of John's life, I literally watched him shrink. He became physically half the size he had been at the beginning of the year. His energy went from fair to crappy to non-existent. By the time he got ready for the day, he was done for the day. Energy expended and exhausted. As his energy waned, his world began to shrink. There were times when he didn't even have the energy to watch a show on television—let alone go out anywhere. The less he did, the more he went inside himself. His big, positive, happy, never-met-a-stranger personality began shrinking as well. It was the most painful thing I had ever watched.

We knew his time was growing short so everything we did came with a feeling of "the last time." Certainly the Christmas holiday of 2015 held that energy for all of us. In early January 2016, we took a trip to the mountains in Western Washington for a change of pace—to a charming Bavarian-style town called Leavenworth. I wanted to see if we could create just one more memorable trip to add to so many others from the past six and a half years. I packed. I drove. I unpacked. He barely had enough energy to walk to the room.

As we cuddled in bed that night, I said to him, "This is the last hotel room we'll share." He nodded solemnly and I swallowed the lump in my throat. He kept saying, "It's just the two of us," but as I lay in bed watching TV and listening to him sleep, I thought, *No, it's the three of us. You, me, and the uninvited guest who has invaded every moment of our lives for the past two and a half years.* He barely had enough energy to get dressed the next morning. We ended up walking about two blocks up the main street in town (with rests in between) and then ended our weekend trip a day early and drove the three hours home.

During those last months, it felt like I had two emotions. I was either angry or sad. When I was angry, it was at the cancer and the loss of what I thought would be my life and future. When I was sad, I cried a lot. For seemingly no reason, but for so many reasons. It was hard for him and I did my best not to do it when I was around him, but I was rarely successful. I told him how much I missed him, because he was so focused on just making it through every day that there was usually nothing left over for me or anyone else. He told me he missed me too. That absolutely killed me.

He started to wonder what it would feel like to die, how it would happen for him. One day he said to me, "I don't know what that will be like, but I'm guessing I'll just eventually go to sleep and not wake up. I'm just so sorry about how hard it will be for all of you."

Part of me wanted him to be free of the pain and exhaustion the cancer raging through his body was causing. The other part wanted to hang on to him so tightly that he could never leave. I knew he was fighting the same emotions.

On January 19th, 2016, John officially went on hospice. They delivered a walker and a hospital bed, and we had our first visit with Sherri—the amazing hospice nurse who would walk us through the final weeks of John's life. He was still very much alive and feeling optimistic that he still had quite a bit of time left. As I look back on it now, I think it was a big relief to him (even if only subconsciously) to be moving into this last phase of his very long cancer journey. There was nothing left for him to do, no "next thing" that promised to maybe give him back his life. There was no research to do, no action to take. He had permission now to just be, to connect, and to see his life out in the way he wanted to.

I began to notice a shift in all of us. For the first time in two years, we were not strictly focused on his cancer (beyond keeping him comfortable). We all began to accept that the fight was over, and we started letting ourselves focus on his life and all of our wonderful memories of time spent together—the funny stories we'd all heard him tell a dozen times or more—and made sure to say "I love you" to each other over and over again. For the first ten days that he was on hospice, it was almost like a big, amazing goodbye party, with people coming to visit, laughing, eating, and—most of all—loving on him. He sat in the middle of that party smiling pretty much non-stop. We had to almost force him to rest, and to sleep now and then because he didn't want to miss anything.

I told him one morning that they should put the words, "What can I do for you?" on his headstone because he was always thinking of what he could do to support others. His love language was acts of service. He said to me numerous times over the course of the next three weeks (often through a Fentanyl-induced haze), "I just want to make sure you have everything you need."

Amidst the awfulness of watching the most important person in your life die in a hospital bed in your dining room, there are gifts and there is sweetness. We looked for those individually and as a family. We danced around death, surrounding John with love and laughter and tears. There was the delicious, normal, everyday chaos of dogs barking, food being prepared in the kitchen off the dining room, people laughing, and the TV on in the background. And he was so happy to be in the center of it all—sometimes asleep, sometimes resting his eyes and listening, always a presence for all of us.

I hadn't realized until those weeks what an impact John had made with his life. He left a legacy of love as he departed that still inspires me when I think back on it. He had visitors from all of the periods in his life—from high school friends to old girlfriends (one of whom drove the 350 miles from Seattle just to spend an hour with him and say goodbye), to work friends and friends we'd met together, as well as close and far-away family. Our friend Chuck (who lived in our motorhome for three short months in 2011 while he was here working at a winery) felt so strongly about saying goodbye that he flew all the way from Tampa, Florida just to spend a few days with John. We were inundated with messages of love and memories of good times spent together. You could see who John was—the imprint he was leaving on so many—in this outpouring of love.

His physical appearance changed drastically every day. I remember the intake day with his hospice nurse, when she looked at John sitting in a chair in our living room and said, "I'd say you have several weeks, possibly even a few months." A week later when she visited, she was shocked at his decline. She estimated that he'd lost at least twenty pounds in less than a week. He had no fat left and his muscle tissue was being consumed by the cancer daily. Since his stomach had been completely closed off by the huge tumor on his duodenum by the end of January, he was no longer absorbing anything he ate (via mouth or feeding tube) and she told us that any nutrition that did somehow manage to get through would only be used by the cancer to make more cancer. We surrendered to that and he stopped eating.

As the pain increased, so did the pain meds which made him fairly lethargic (something he hated). We worked every day to manage his pain without over-medicating him to the point where he couldn't experience his life. Most days, we did a pretty good job of it. He remained ambulatory, choosing to get up, shower, shave, and put on cologne ("So I smell like myself for you guys") every day. He got weaker by the day and after the first week, we never let him get up and walk without someone shadowing him in case his legs gave out. It was important to him to "show up" for his life and for us and to maintain as much of a normal routine as possible, for as long as possible.

Most importantly, we just spent time with him. Oddly enough, that very difficult time also felt like a blessing. John was still there, could still hear what we needed to tell him and say what he needed to say. It was a gift that many people don't get and we were all keenly aware of that. There was nothing left unsaid. We talked a lot about what would happen when he did finally pass. We promised him we would surround him with our love for the last time and release him on his journey. He kept telling us he would just be "in the next room," not gone but just not here in the way we had always known him. He was not afraid to die.

He told me on the day they delivered the hospital bed that it was important to him to sleep upstairs in our bed at night as long as he could get up and down the stairs. In the quiet evening hour before bed, when all of the company had gone, our family would gather, sit on his hospice bed, lie next to him, pull up chairs, and share. We told stories and laughed, asked questions and listened, shared sorrows and cried. We were there for him. We were there for each other.

When it was time for bed, everyone would gather around him and basically "push" him up the stairs to our bedroom. Then, one by one, they'd hug him, tell him goodnight and leave us alone. That time was so precious to all of us, especially him. The first night it happened, he woke up in the middle of the night to tell me how much he loved it and how important it was to him.

For me, it was our own private time at bedtime, after the kids had gone and first thing in the morning before he went downstairs that was more precious than gold, the quiet talks and tender touches feeding my memory for a lifetime. I cried a lot during these private moments and he held me, loving me through my grief without words, because there was nothing to say.

We have an app on our phones called Life360 that our family uses to keep track of each other. It's a GPS app that tells us where everybody is at any given moment. We always teased John about "creeping" on that app, stalking us, especially when one of us was traveling or out of town. One night as we were going to bed, I opened it to see where my son Eli was and said to him, "I wish they could put heaven on here so I can see where you are once you're gone." He pointed to the spot on the map that was our house and said to me, "It's already there."

The last three nights before we stopped having John sleep upstairs with me, it got harder and harder for me because he was up every hour. He needed bandages changed, his feeding tube drained, and sometimes changes of clothes. I just wasn't getting enough sleep to make it through the emotionally and physically draining days of taking care of him and fitting in work, here and there, when I could.

I finally had to surrender to the fact that I couldn't keep going without sleep and I asked for help. I knew that meant he wouldn't be coming upstairs to our bedroom or sleeping in our bed again, so it was a really tough decision for me. He started sleeping in the hospital bed downstairs at night and his brother and kids stepped in to take night duty. I had to relinquish control, and trust others with his care for the first time, which was really challenging for me.

I'd been his sole caregiver since the day he was diagnosed. It had been two and a half years and, at times, was a full-time job. I realized in those final few weeks that my caregiver role had defined so much of my life that I wasn't sure who I'd be without it. His needs, his care—especially in the last six months of his life—had taken much of my time and attention. That caregiving had woven itself into my daily routine. I realized that once he was gone, there would be a huge chunk of my purpose that would go with him.

I worked a little here and there, but I honestly didn't get much accomplished. There were his medical needs (which were significant) and the fact that whenever I was in my office working—even though I could see him from there—I felt like I needed to be next to him instead. I listened to that intuitive push. I spent hours just sitting and holding his hand or lying with him and cuddling, talking, laughing and crying.

Up until almost the very end, John remained more concerned about everyone around him than he was about himself. Just when I thought he'd given all he could, he would surprise us with more. He grew tired of fighting, tired of the pain, but he never tired of making sure we knew how much he loved us. Three days before he died, during our late night family time, he told us we were his core and had us all pose for a picture that he took from his hospice bed.

The final days of John's life were like a roller coaster. John was down to around seventy-five pounds. He started having more pain and being more out of it than with it—one foot in this world and one in the next. On the Wednesday night before the Sunday he died, he called us all together and told us he thought he'd be going soon. He said he really didn't want many more days like that day. He told us how much he loved us and that he believed, somehow, once he passed he'd be able to watch over all of us all at once. We all cried a lot and hugged and told him we were ok and that he could go, that we'd take care of each other.

The next day he was sleeping a lot and then, out of the blue, he was suddenly wide awake, lucid and energetic, and decided he wanted to go outside. We carried him out to the back porch and he sat breathing the fresh air. He was laughing and happy, but told us again that night that he felt his time was near. He didn't close his eyes during those final days—even when he slept—so it was hard to know where he was. He was such a communicator his whole life, so to not know what he was feeling or experiencing was a real challenge. We wanted to help him but didn't know what was going on and he couldn't tell us. I believe he was fighting the transition because of all of the love he was receiving and the love that he felt for us. He just couldn't let go.

It dawned on me that the greatest lessons he taught me during our life together had been about patience, and he was the most patient person I ever knew. I had to accept the fact that he would wait patiently (and ask us to do the same) until the time was right and he was ready. All I wanted was a peaceful transition for him but selfishly, I was ready for the ride to end. I was bone tired, humbled, honored, and heartbroken as we approached the end. I wondered how I would ever find normal again without my beloved.

The day John died was one of those rare warm beautiful sunny winter days in Walla Walla, Washington. It was Superbowl Sunday, February 7th, 2016. I stood by his hospice bed and watched the sun rise from the window in our living room from which he'd watched the world for almost three weeks. I don't remember if it was a beautiful sunrise. If so, the beauty did not register for me. What I do remember was thinking that this was the day I would lose the love of my life.

It had been a difficult forty-eight hours. John did not succumb peacefully and easily to death. He didn't want to die and he clung to life with every ounce of energy he had left. The morning before—as his kids and I sat with him—he had become very agitated and very emotional, clinging to the bed rails, literally and figuratively holding on. He didn't seem to really know we were there and twice his face crumpled up and he cried, "I don't want to go. I know I have to go but I don't want to go."

He used what was left of his conscious energy that day to wake up and say goodbye to his older brother and family when they visited and, by early evening, he was in an unresponsive coma. I remember panicking a little, wondering if I'd said everything I needed to say to him because now it was too late. Then, as we changed his clothes and his twin brother took his shirt off over his head, suddenly he was there. He looked at me with that incredible smile that seemed always present and his eyes danced with love and recognition. "Well hi there!" I said, amazed and thrilled.

"Hi beautiful," he said as I held his hand. And then he was gone again.

Those were the last words he ever said. Even though he didn't actually pass away for another sixteen hours, I believe that was the moment when his soul moved on. I never felt his presence after that instant. He just wasn't "there" anymore, even though he was still breathing and his heart still continued to beat. It was a gift that he gave me, one final gift, that has stayed with me and sustained me hundreds of times since that moment.

I remember standing at his bedside at 3:00 a.m. on the day that he died. I'd been snoozing on the couch, half conscious of his labored breathing and waiting for it to stop. Everyone else was asleep and I had thought (as I drifted off), that he would probably choose to pass once he was alone, knowing we wouldn't have to experience that moment and wanting to spare us all. I remember being surprised when I awoke to hear his uneven, ragged breathing.

I watched him for a few moments, barely recognizing the skeletal figure in the bed as the man who had changed my life and loved me so fiercely and perfectly. His eyes were open, as they had been continuously for the past several days. It was eerie and disturbing to know he wasn't seeing anything out of them. I took his hand, pressed it to my cheek and said, "Babe, you've got to let go. We need you to let go. I don't know how much more of this we can take. It's ok for you to go now. We love you and we want you to go."

I wanted to scream in frustration. I just wanted it to end. It felt like the only thing I wanted in that moment was for it to end, for it all—PLEASE GOD—to just be over. And he kept right on breathing. I remember when he finally drew his last breath, feeling an overwhelming sense of relief and in the very next moment, unimaginable agony as I realized he was really gone. I've never wanted—and dreaded—something so much in my entire life. I remember sitting on the stairs, comforting his beautiful daughter Chelsey and finally letting it all go and sobbing for what seemed like hours—two and a half years of pent up anguish finally spilling out of me in waves of grief.

On that bright, shiny morning when he died, I followed his body out of the house as they loaded it into the funeral home minivan. I sat down on the front stairs next to John's son Chad and watched it drive away, fingering his wedding ring on my thumb. I sat there for a long time, paralyzed and feeling like I could not go back into our house. Because he wasn't there.

I knew, when I walked through that door, it would be alone. Without him. I knew that for the rest of my life nothing would ever be the same. Everything I thought I knew about my life was gone. Because he was gone.

CHAPTER 6

WHAT JOHN AND HIS CANCER TAUGHT ME

Before I start this chapter, I'd like to invite you to breathe a collective sigh of relief with me. We've made it through the toughest part of this story. It was a pretty difficult journey and I'm honored that you have taken it this far with me. I promise, things get better in part two (not immediately, but certainly eventually). It took me quite a while to write part one of this book because it was like reliving all the pain from those awful two and a half years. I made a plan to start writing several times in the three years after John died and just couldn't bring myself to do it. Once I finished part one, I understood why. As I edited it after I wrote it, I remember thinking, "This is a pretty depressing book." It concerned me a bit but I also realized that I couldn't share the THRIVE process without telling the whole, brutally painful story of John's cancer experience and death.

John's cancer journey and loving him through it changed me profoundly and in so many different ways. Here's what that incredibly painful and difficult time taught me...

- If there's someone in your life toward whom you're holding a grudge... forgive them.

- If there's something you're holding on to that's making you feel angry, sad, upset, anxious, fearful— or any other negative emotion—LET IT GO.

- If there's someone you've lost touch with (for whatever reason) who was once a positive influence in your life, reach out to them.

- If petty little shit upsets you or sends you off the deep end, stop sweating the small stuff.

- Someday is today. Don't wait.

- Tell the people in your life how important they are to you.

- Hug it out. Then hug it out again.

- Say "I love you" even if you think everyone in your life already knows you love them. Say it tonight. Say it often.

- Finally, shut down your email and computer, turn off the TV, put down your cell phone and INTERACT with your family.

By the end of his second week on hospice, we turned off the television and rarely had it on. We shut off our phones and only checked them a few times a day. No one missed either. It forced us to talk—to each other and to him. We were more present and there for each other because the background noise was turned off. It was such a gift and it made our final days with John more sacred.

I let go of worry about work or money, knowing that his life and making sure he got to see it out in his way with all of us around him, was far more important. I can always work, can always earn money, I'll always be fine. What mattered during this time was my other priorities.

You may be a workaholic like I was—constantly available to your customers or team, or incessantly checking email or Facebook on your smartphone when you're supposed to be present with your family and loved ones.

Stop it.

NOTHING you'll see on any screen is as important as the people who are right in front of you. Create time to work and then put it away and invest yourself in those around you. Because—trust me when I tell you—they can be gone in the blink of an eye and you'll never regret any time you spent with them.

If I could have just one more day, one more hour, one more minute with my beloved John, I'd give up anything for it. The finality of his absence from my life still knocks the wind out of me sometimes—even years later. He really is not coming back and the memories we shared—memories I made by stepping away from my business and into our lives—are ones I will cherish. I have no regrets about putting my business on the back burner and feel blessed that I was able to do that.

The bottom line is that life really is short and you will never regret living in the moment, following an impulse, and seizing the day. John totally "got" this too. During those final weeks, as I would be busily and efficiently taking care of him—changing a bandage, helping him change his clothes, or getting him out of the shower—he would stop, make me look at him, hold me, and take a moment to just love me and force me to slow down and feel it. Those moments are the ones I treasure.

I was loved so excellently, completely, and unconditionally by this incredible man. He continually informed my sometimes-insecure self of my worth, empowered me to walk through the world knowing how loved I was, and emboldened me after his death to hold out for the perfect relationship—of which he knew I was worthy. He taught me how I was supposed to be loved, by others and by myself.

That knowledge would make the next part of this very difficult journey a learning experience I never expected. It would inform how I showed up in the months after John died, and who I became in the ensuing years.

PART 2

JULIE

A REBIRTH STORY

CHAPTER 7

HOW WILL I GO ON?

John died on February 7th, 2016, Superbowl Sunday, at 10:27 a.m. Our NFL team, the Seattle Seahawks, who had been to the Superbowl during the previous two years, had missed it in 2016, eliminated during the conference playoffs. Nonetheless, John had made a vow that he'd be here for Superbowl Sunday. More importantly, his daughter Chelsey's birthday was on February 1st, my son Sam's was on the 3rd, and my nephew Cameron's was on the 6th. I really believe getting through all of those milestone days without tainting them for the rest of our lives and keeping his promise to make it to the Superbowl fueled his final few days. He'd always been one hundred percent true to his word and leaving this world was no exception.

I remember having the TV on that afternoon after he died—not invested in the game but not sure what else to do in the wake of his body leaving our home earlier that day. I sat in my big leather chair, reading the comments and texts flooding my phone, taking some comfort in the love and support from thousands of Facebook "friends" who had been on this journey with us and felt John's loss even though they'd never officially met him. At the end of the Superbowl halftime show, the audience participated in a card stunt, creating a rainbow and the phrase "Believe in love"—the closing lyrics to Coldplay's "A Head Full of Dreams." Since we'd been using the hashtag #lovetrumpscancer, it felt like a sign.

Then I got a very clear, intuitive hit to check my text history. I scrolled down to the last texts from John. There were a few from the first week he'd been on hospice when I'd actually been away from him for an hour or so at a time (but not many more), as we'd been together twenty-four seven for the final few weeks of his life. I scrolled back to our last actual conversation and this text came into view...

John: Just above you.

Me: What! Can you see me?

John: I think so.

It was from a few weeks earlier as I was driving back from the airport after a trip to Florida to speak, and he was treated to a helicopter ride by one of his clients. He had flown above my car.

As I looked at that text, I got a chill. I could feel John there, hovering over me, loving me, there with me. It was the first of many times that's happened since he died. I still get "nudges" from him quite frequently. Never one quite as clear as that one, however. I have no doubt that he was, indeed, "just above me" and that knowledge carried me through the day.

If you've never suffered a profound loss, it's hard to really imagine how intensely painful it is. In the days after John's death I experienced unbelievable—almost unbearable— sadness mixed with sweet moments with good friends and family, laughing at things he would have said and crying because I would never hear him say certain things again. During those first few weeks, I woke up every morning thinking—just for an instant, in that hazy, in between place of sleeping and waking—that he was still beside me. I longed with all my might for it to be true—grief replacing that instant of hope, once I became fully conscious. Every morning I would get out of a bed that was completely undisturbed on one side and face, again, the inescapable singleness of that act. I constantly wondered how I could possibly live another day without him. I witnessed the reality that he was really, truly NEVER coming back start to sink in, like a pebble slowly spiraling to the bottom of a lake.

The first week after his death was one of firsts and lasts. I found myself floating in unfamiliar water, doing my best to navigate the rough parts and most often, just barely keeping my head above the waves. I felt incomplete and alone and lost. Mostly, I wanted some semblance of "normal" back in my life but I was also keenly aware that I was not ready for it yet. So I just had to accept that my job—my only job—was to grieve.

I made the choice to "lean in" to every emotion, allowing it to take me away, not fighting or feeling the need to control like I normally would. I held no expectations around how I would feel in ten minutes, two hours or tomorrow. It was all new territory. I felt adrift in this sea of grief with no shore in sight, and not even an oar to steer with (because that's where I had to be). It was terrifying and inevitable and there was nothing to be done about it except to float. There was no action I could take to speed it along or stop it. No plans I could make about my life or my future. For the first time ever, I realized that I was just supposed to drift and be sure to hang on during the rough, scary parts.

There were flower deliveries and sympathy cards and messages of support and love designed to distract me from the pain. There were meals dropped off and kind acts done designed to help where no help was really possible. In the midst of all of my pain, the practical side of death had to be dealt with. There were arrangements to be made, people to inform, insurance companies to call, obituaries to be written, and his final tribute to plan. I made three trips to the funeral home in the first week after he died and every time, it felt surreal—like I was watching someone I didn't know (but who looked exactly like me) in a really sad movie.

As the time passed, there were short (and far too infrequent) periods of happiness, boredom, or laughter—but mostly, everything was a reminder that he was gone and never coming back. Because John and I had practically been joined at the hip, (especially in the last year of his illness) there was virtually no place I could go that didn't bring back a flood of memories, that didn't make me yearn for him.

I also felt lost and very alone, even though my house was still full of people. All of a sudden, and in that instant that John passed, I had lost most of my identity. I didn't know who I was. Suddenly, I wasn't a wife or a caregiver or a partner. Even though I was still a mom and a stepmom, my kids were all grown up. Sure, they still needed me, but they were adults with lives of their own.

This was supposed to be our time. We had plans for what we would do once Eli (my youngest) graduated from high school that June. Now, I was on my own. I didn't have any immediate responsibility for anyone but myself and my dog. I could go anywhere, do anything, be anyone I wanted to be. The opportunities were endless. I remember sharing my fears about my future with my stepdaughter Chelsey one night, not long after John passed. She told me to look at it like an adventure. She said that's what her dad would tell me to do and I knew she was right.

But right then, in the sad days after he passed, it just felt incredibly overwhelming, sad, and honestly—terrifying. The one person who completed me (as cliché as that sounds), who totally understood me and wanted to take this adventure with me, was gone. For good. Nothing I did, no amount of wishing or praying, was going to bring him back. People kept telling me that he was still with me, would always be with me, and to just "get quiet" and I'd feel him. But I was in too much pain for that. No matter how hard I tried to connect with him, the reality was, he just felt gone.

There's a quote that says that there's no such thing as safe love. Real love is giving someone the power to hurt you. John never hurt me while he was alive, but having loved him as deeply and profoundly as I did, his death hurt more than I ever imagined it would. I know John and I had an incredible love that most people don't ever get and that made us very lucky. Amazingly, I even realized how special it was while he was loving me, which was a huge gift. In the years since he died, that's become a source of comfort and happiness to me. But in the days and weeks after he passed, it just made me hurt more because, as the reality and finality of the fact that he was gone began to take root for me, I also became keenly aware of what I had lost.

CHAPTER 8

DIVING INTO GRIEF

John's celebration of life service happened two weeks after he died, on a beautiful, sunny winter day in Walla Walla. It was nothing short of magical. The love that was present for the entire day was life-affirming and I felt completely wrapped in that love, and supported by all of the amazing people from John's life and my own—some of whom traveled thousands of miles to be there. It was an entire twelve hours (at least) of TRUE celebration.

The service was exactly what John wanted (and planned out before he died). Right down to the end of the video and the theme song from *The Golden Girls* ("Thank You For Being A Friend") that he requested we use, to the colorful, balloon-filled reception orchestrated by our sweet friend Lynnette. His hand was present (just like his loving energy) in the entire day.

I wrote, rehearsed, and delivered a heartfelt eulogy of our life and love. It was easier than I thought it would be. Someone actually told me at the reception that it was interesting to see me step into "speaker mode" since they'd never seen me speak before. I hadn't realized that's what I'd done until the speech was over. I walked back to my seat, sat down between my boys, and pretty much wept through the rest of the service. But once it was done, there were no more tears for the rest of the day. Just connection, stories shared, love, and laughter. It was absolutely magical and beautiful.

At the end of the night, as the celebration at our home was winding down (and the over fifty people who crammed into our cozy house filtered out), I realized that the divine, magical, positive, loving vibe from the day was just like the energy of our vow renewal weekend the previous Labor Day—there was nothing but love.

The two weeks between John's death and his memorial service were incredibly hard but not as hard, I'd soon learn, as the days to come once the distraction of having something to focus on and people around all the time were gone.

I've had my heart broken dozens of times in my life. I've been through two painful divorces, said goodbye to lovers and friends when things didn't work out, cried painful tears over those losses, and moved on with my life. My heartbreak recovery time was about six weeks to three months, depending upon the gravity of the breakup, but the really bad grief of those losses never lasted more than a few weeks.

What I came to realize after John's death was that there is loss, and then there is the absolute, no-going-back, *forever* loss of your best friend and soulmate. Nothing I'd ever been through before had prepared me for this loss. Knowing it was probably coming for at least eighteen months and then definitely coming for five before John died made not one iota of difference in the moment he passed. I had thought I was at least a little bit prepared. I was wrong.

This heartbreak was physical. When it hit—like a rogue wave crashing over me and pushing me under—it was physical and emotional. A visceral experience like none I'd ever had. There was no rhythm to this sea. I never knew when a storm would come up and I'd be tossed about again, and moments could spring up throughout the day that startled me in their unexpected intensity.

Moments like opening the favorites tab on my phone for the first time and seeing John's smiling face and number at the top of the list. Walking into our favorite Mexican restaurant with my kids and almost running out in a panic of grief at the memories. Making phone calls to close accounts and remove him from insurance policies and choking on the words, "my husband passed away last week." Bursting into tears at the urgent care counter when the receptionist asked me who my emergency contact was.

Like an out of control toddler prone to tantrums, grief controlled my life—it frustrated and often embarrassed me. I had always been a person who was in control and had a plan. There was no room for control or planning inside of (what an article I read at the time called) "complicated grief". It said that dealing with grief was like immigrating to a foreign country where you don't speak the language. For me, it went deeper. Sometimes it felt like being teleported to a different planet where I couldn't even breathe the air.

It reminds me of a quote from the book *The Secret Life of Bees*, "It is the peculiar nature of the world to go on spinning no matter what sort of heartbreak is happening." As my mom always says, "life goes on." And that was the problem. While my neighbors walked their dogs and fellow shoppers pushed their carts around the grocery store like everything was normal, I wanted to scream at them for not realizing that nothing was normal.

Everything was hard and nothing was normal. Life as I knew it literally ended when John drew his final breath. He was my life and I defined so much of myself and the way I showed up in this world based on our relationship. Now I had to start over amidst the pain of knowing he was gone. I had to somehow come up with a plan for my life going forward. It was uncharted territory and I had to find my way without the benefit of the one person I trusted to help steer me. His imprint on my life was so deep that I truly couldn't imagine moving forward without him walking beside me.

I realized that I had to learn to trust myself completely, knowing that the person I became because of the way he loved me was capable of moving forward. I had to be ok with not knowing what the future would hold and letting it unfold naturally as I worked my way through that ocean of grief.

In the first months after John died I also found myself arguing with reality—floating in this strange, in between world of what I knew to be true, and what my grieving self refused to believe was true. I'd have totally irrational thoughts like, "I have to remember to tell John about the brakes on the car," or be out shopping and put something in my cart I knew he loved to eat. It wasn't that I forgot he was dead, it was that my mind seemed to be literally rejecting that reality at times.

I had some pretty scary dreams during that period of time as well where that same juxtaposition of what I knew to be true and what I wanted to be true confused and frightened me. In the dreams, I could never reach him and he was usually in peril or, worse, dead. I'd dream that he was drowning and that I couldn't reach him, watching his body swept away down a raging river, while at the same time thinking, "He can't be drowning. His ashes are in a cardboard box in the coat closet downstairs." It was pretty disconcerting, but not unusual for someone grieving the loss of someone they loved.

The first time I traveled by air was about three weeks after John died. I traveled a lot, mostly for work, during the first four years of our relationship before he got sick (and some after he was diagnosed as well). When I was traveling, he was my anchor, someone who tracked my progress and with whom I checked in before each takeoff and landing. He was the one I called at the end of the day, sharing all of my adventures and hearing about the mundane, ordinary things that happened at home when I wasn't there. We never went to bed without saying I love you, even when I was sleeping in a different time zone.

After he died, I didn't just miss being with him, I missed knowing who I was in the world even when I wasn't with him. I picked up the phone to call or text him at least a dozen times a week in the month after he died. He wasn't just my love and my husband, he was also my best friend and the first one I always wanted to share everything with. So I felt very lost and very sad.

Worse, everyone kept telling me that he was still with me, that he was walking beside me every minute. I wanted to believe that more than anything in the world, but there was no evidence that he was there—no signs recognized or overwhelming feelings of his presence. No feathers raining down from heaven or random birds or butterflies.

I realized that I was also getting to know a new version of myself I'd never met before. I've never been a sad person. I've never had a lot of patience for sad people. I've always powered through and, as my mom would say, "pulled myself up by my bootstraps" and carried on. I'd have gotten over it and focused on what's next. If there's one thing that became clear to me during those first few months after John's death, it was that

I was not going to be getting over this anytime soon. So I realized that I better just relax and be ok with being sad.

I did my best to stick to a weekly routine, hoping my life would feel a bit more like normal again, but no amount of structure could erase the sadness. Some days that meant I couldn't actually stick to my plans because I just couldn't bring myself to work out, or go to lunch, or create a landing page that day, and I had to be ok with that. Old me was rapidly introduced to the new (temporary) me.

I'd been told and read that the beginning of the grieving process was the most difficult and painful part and that, because of that, many people tend to do anything they can to avoid it. Ignoring their feelings or distracting themselves instead of embracing the pain. Doing that doesn't make the intense first stages of grief go away, it just postpones it. It's like being stuck in a traffic circle, going past your exit over and over again, afraid to actually move to the right and take it. You may feel less stress while you're going around the opposite side of the circle, but eventually that same exit comes around again—bringing the anxiety and fear right along with it.

That perpetual cycle wasn't for me. I knew that even before John died. I made a conscious decision to take the exit on the first loop. I dove into grief headfirst, employing the first two steps in the THRIVE process, trusting myself and honoring my feelings. I made a few strategic decisions that not everyone makes that I believe made all the difference for me.

First, I sought out support in every form possible. I read books people recommended. I availed myself of the hospice counselor who reached out to me. I joined a local grief support group and went every single week. I even found an online support group and joined that.

Second, I leaned into the feelings, no matter where I was or what was happening. I cried gallons of tears and lost myself for the better part of three months. My main goal was to get through the worst of the grieving as quickly as possible while still staying totally present to that work and letting it take as long as it took.

I blogged throughout John's entire cancer journey, right up until the day he died, and for a few years after. I shared the facts and the ups and downs of living with a terminal illness. I shared my own thoughts and feelings, and the changes I was experiencing because of our journey. And because of the power of our love, the blog became a love story that people resonated with.

During one of my meetings with a grief counselor at hospice I was telling her about the *Love Trumps Cancer* blog and what that meant to us, that as long as we focused on love, cancer couldn't win. She said something that really made sense but that I hadn't thought of before. She said she believed that the grieving process is a love story in and of itself, that the more deeply you love someone, the more profoundly you feel their loss when you lose them. The love I felt for John informed the sometimes all-consuming grief I was feeling. I couldn't have one without the other.

The last thing I said as I ended John's eulogy at his memorial service was that if, on that first day I fell in love with him, he'd told me that we'd only get six and a half years, I would have jumped in headfirst with just as much enthusiasm and abandon as I did without that knowledge. If I hadn't loved him so much, I wouldn't have been such a mess during the months after he died. There was something about that realization, about thinking of the grieving process as a continuation of our love story, that helped immensely.

CHAPTER 9

LOSING MYSELF

I grew up Episcopalian and during Lent, all of the celebration was deleted from the liturgy. In all the places where we said "hallelujah" during the rest of the year, the word was left out. I vividly remember my relief on Easter Sunday when the proclamation was back where it belonged in the familiar liturgy that I knew by heart, and I could joyfully and deliberately declare it once again. It meant that the dark weeks of Lent were over, the light and happiness flooded back in, and anything seemed possible.

I believe that's the perfect metaphor for the first stages of grief. Lent is a time where life goes on but with an overarching sadness and sacrifice that seems to permeate everything. It's why Easter is such a celebration, such a relief.

For me, those first months felt exactly the same way. It was as if all of the "hallelujahs" had been removed from my life. I got up, showed up, and walked through my day, sometimes with a face that defied what I was actually feeling inside. I exercised, put on makeup, worked, cooked, cleaned, and laughed at people's jokes. But it was all done without celebration. I was constantly looking for joy, and most of the time I remembered it had died (at least temporarily) when John died.

Sometimes I felt ok, and little glimmers of hope would seep in, but then another wave of unexpected sadness would hit and I'd be back at ground zero again. It was a pretty exhausting process, all in all, and most of the time I would have rather been anywhere than where I was, without John.

The thing about Lent is that there's a defined end to it. You know you can circle Easter Sunday on the calendar and look forward to the celebration. If you give something up for Lent, you know it's temporary. You literally see the light at the end of the tunnel. Not so with grief. It's why grieving is so hard, because there's no way of knowing when you'll feel true joy again, when you'll feel like you're in control again. I was plugging back in and walking through my life knowing it would happen—but not knowing when it would happen was a foreign and very difficult thing.

I remember about a month after John died, I woke up to overcast skies and drying pavement after a few days of rain. Feeling optimistic, I leashed up my pup Lucy and we set off. Within minutes it started sprinkling, but just a little. About a mile in, the wind kicked up and it started to rain. Just a little at first, but then really hard. Before I knew it, it was raining sideways, the wind blowing big, hard raindrops against my face and skin. I was over a mile away from home and there was nothing I could do but finish my walk.

I was miserable. Cold, wet, and feeling helpless with only a few choices. I could see if I could find a tree or awning, take cover, and wait out the squall (but who knew how long that would take), or I could just put my head down, weather the storm, and walk as fast as possible toward home.

It struck me as a pretty accurate metaphor for my life in that moment. Things seemed ok for a minute, and then the wind would kick up and the deluge of grief would start pummeling me. I was helpless against it and there was nowhere to run. The only choice was to walk as fast as I could through the downpour until I reached shelter and could find a bit of my dry center again.

That stormy day, once I got home, I peeled off my soaking wet clothes, got into a nice hot shower, and sobbed. Because I was so lonely. Because I missed him so much. Because I had no idea where to run or what to do to feel better. Because it felt like all of my memories were with him and I couldn't stop them from flooding in every minute of every day. Because, in those first few months, those memories brought more pain than joy. Because my happy place was him and I had no idea where to look for it once he was gone.

I wanted a timeline, like Easter after Lent. I wanted to circle a date on the calendar and know that I would only feel that completely horrible until then and after that, getting out of bed would be easy again. I wanted to feel true happiness for even one minute again, to somehow find a way to climb out from under that overwhelming blanket of sadness, and dance in the rain instead of just miserably getting through it.

Intellectually I knew there was no timeline and that eventually a little joy would start to seep back in, a drop at a time. But my heart did not understand.

People have always told me I'm one of the strongest people they know. Before losing John, I used to brush off those words, saying things like, "I'm no stronger than anyone else. I'm just loud." I don't do that anymore. I'm damn strong, and I got through something so painful and horrible that some people never really recover from it.

But it took a lot longer to begin to feel like myself again than anyone ever knew. I know I appeared strong and made it seem like everything was ok in my new world without John. I presented that face to the world pretty much from the beginning of my grief journey. It was easy for the people around me to convince themselves that I was "back to normal." I even had someone ask me, a few months after John died, if I was better now. I looked him dead in the eye and said bluntly, "No. I'm not better. At all." Just because I wasn't crying most of the day anymore didn't mean I wasn't still in intense pain.

I think people NEEDED me to be ok so they could feel fine about things getting back to "normal" in our relationship. So many close friends were there for me in the few months before John died, helping out, checking in almost daily, bringing food, and just holding me up. Then, within weeks of his death, they stopped calling and checking in. They asked how I was when we did chat or see each other, but I don't think they really understood my answer and sometimes, it was easier just to say, "I'm hanging in there," and leave it at that. I sensed their discomfort, the fact that they prayed I wouldn't break down because they wouldn't know what to say, or do, to help me.

I didn't blame them, and I knew from what I'd been learning about grieving that it was totally normal for this to happen. But the thing I needed them to know and couldn't articulate was that I was in severe, deep, intense pain. This was, without a doubt, the most difficult thing I had ever been through. My hospice counselor said that, unless you've been through the process of grieving someone whom you loved deeply, you can't really understand what it's like, the intensity of it, or how long it takes to move through it. If people did understand, I wouldn't have spent so much time alone.

I didn't expect anyone to "help" with that pain. There was no way to do that. I just needed to be around people who cared about me. I was feeling isolated. I was spending too much time alone and it was not good for me. I needed support but I didn't want to have to ask for it. Reaching out and saying, "Could you invite me to do something or just offer to come hang out with me or call me every day to check in?" felt uncomfortable and most often, even if I had the intention to reach out, it got lost in the exhaustion of grief and I never did.

I know I have amazing friends who love me a lot, but during that time I was no longer "top of mind" for them once a few months had passed. It became clear very quickly that grieving was a singularly lonely act. Not only was I swimming through the deep waters of grief, but I was really doing it on my own for the most part.

While the weekdays were challenging, at least I had work to distract me. But the weekends were long, lonely, and hard. It felt like everyone had a life and people who counted on them, except me. John and I had talked about this very thing before he died. He knew that everyone else in his life, from his kids to his siblings, would have someone there for them, someone to come home to and to live their lives with.

And he knew that I wouldn't. It hurt him because there was nothing he could do about it. He told me more than once that I had the harder job of the two of us, that if he could trade places with me he would. He said he had no idea how he'd survive if I died.

I spend a lot of time alone and I don't really mind being alone—but when it went on for days at a time because my person was gone and everyone else was with their people, it made me miss him even more. I felt like the world had moved on but I was stuck. I would see couples out and about, on

Facebook, or on TV and I just wanted to scream because they had what I didn't have anymore—and they had no idea how fragile it was.

If you have a significant other, count yourself blessed. It means there's someone there in the middle of the night to soothe you if you have a nightmare. It means you have someone to share everything with, from meals to walks in the park. It means you always have a date on Friday night. It means there's someone in the world who's always thinking about you, sometimes worrying about you, and who always has your back. Someone to make plans with and whose needs you consider before you make decisions about your life.

Don't ever take your partner for granted. That connection is priceless and the world can be a really lonely place without it.

When John was alive, it seemed like we were always on an adventure, always surrounded by fun. Most of the time it was just the two of us but I felt complete, whole. It dawned on me that, after he died, it felt like I was a small percentage of who I had been with him. Not just half of me felt gone. Most of me felt gone.

But how was that possible? The math didn't work. How could one person exiting my life feel this lonely. Nothing else had changed. I still had four kids, a loving, supportive family, and great friends. But after his death, the pervading feeling in my life was loneliness. No matter who I was with or what I was doing, I felt lonely.

I remember visiting John's gravestone a few months after he died. I stood there in that surreal place in that surreal moment and said to my friend, "I certainly never imagined I'd be here at this point in my life."

Here being alone. After having found the perfect love of my life at the perfect time in my life. And then losing him too soon. It felt brutal and so painful it's unimaginable. How could he have been so "in" my life one minute and then just gone the next?

Even a change of scenery didn't help. I took my youngest son Eli to Hawaii for spring break, about two months after John died. He was a senior in high school and about to graduate and move out on his own, so I thought this would be an awesome opportunity to spend some quality time with him while I still could. I also felt like some happy sunshine would be good for both of us (but especially me).

The last time I had gone to Hawaii had been with John. We had a wonderful vacation in Maui the year before he was diagnosed. We loved being together and were active vacationers. We parasailed, paddle boarded, snorkeled, and took a sunset dinner cruise. We rented a car and drove all over the island. It was an amazing week.

Even though Eli and I were on a different island, it still felt a little too familiar. We spent a day touring museums and exhibits at Pearl Harbor and Ford Island, rented a car and drove to the North Shore, chilled on the beach, and had a great time.

Except there was a pervasive sadness over the week for me. Nothing dramatic, just around the edges of the days and especially the nights. I'm still glad we went. It just didn't feel a whole lot different from being anywhere else. Without John. Because no matter where I was, he wasn't there. I kept thinking about how much he would have loved doing and seeing everything we were doing and seeing. And even though I had a great time with my son, I still just missed my best friend and lover. I felt incomplete and lonely without him, no matter who I was with.

The most profound thing I realized through the beginning of my grief was that my relationship with John continued beyond his death and into this new life I was carving out. I began to realize that our relationship would, in fact, never end. It was just different now. I still loved him more than I could even articulate, got frustrated when something came up that he left unfinished that I had to deal with, or reached for the phone to share with him every time something cool happened in my life.

I began to realize that he was, in fact, there with me—always present in my thoughts, through photographs all over my life, and in the small touches and big things he did to make our home ours. So in that sense, the people who had said that to me in the weeks after he died were right.

The other big thing I learned about grieving was that it was a process I just had to be present to and move through. One of the books I read compared it to a journey through a forest. Sometimes dark and scary, and other times beautiful and inspiring. I know I'll never stop grieving and that my job is always to be as present as possible to what I'm feeling, allow myself to experience it in whatever way it manifests, and be gentle with myself through the process.

I stopped waiting for things to "go back to normal" or to feel "normal" again. I began to understand that I would never be the same person I had been before John died but that I was becoming someone different—creating a new normal—through the grieving process.

Although I didn't believe it at the time, now I actually look at my journey and I'm grateful for what it's taught me and the person I've become because of it. There was a time, early on, when I hoped for that but couldn't see the path to that eventuality. Still, I could feel that transformation happening and I grew more and more curious about how my new self would unfold.

CHAPTER 10

FINDING MYSELF

It had been just under four months since John had passed away. Some days it felt much longer and others it felt like yesterday. My sense of "us-ness" began fading a little each day and I found myself grieving that fact in addition to grieving his loss. We were so great together and I missed who I was when I was with him almost as much as I missed him.

I also noticed, the further from his death I got, the more I seemed to "hear" him. I distinctly remember a moment in June when I was dancing with friends and I felt him there with me and heard him whisper in my ear, "YES! This is what I want for you. Grab this joy! You're doing great!" It was a bittersweet moment because it was exactly what he would have said to me if he had been standing right in front of me actually talking to me. It felt very right.

I wanted to move on and hold on, all at the same time. The more "normal" my life got without him, the further away from him I felt. That was a relief in one moment, and sad the next. Regardless, I was still leaning into all of my emotions and allowing myself to feel whatever each moment brought. I stopped feeling guilty for being happy.

As my grief progressed, I learned the difference between grieving and mourning. Grieving is how you feel about the loss on the inside and mourning is how you express the pain of your loss outwardly. It wasn't long before I noticed that my moments of mourning came less frequently and mostly in private. I still had times when tears threatened but I could generally talk myself down off the cliff, especially if I was somewhere in public where it wasn't particularly convenient to break down and sob. A month earlier, I couldn't have done that so it felt like progress.

I also started finding more and more moments of joy. Sometimes, I'd even have hours of joy. I felt more autonomous and was re-learning how to be "just me." It was a hard journey. I never wanted to be single again and had grown very accustomed to being half of a whole, even while John was sick and I was his sole caregiver and the main breadwinner. I got spoiled being in love with my best friend, always having someone there to cheer me on and bounce ideas off. I almost had to learn to trust my own instincts and decisions again. But it began to happen, a little at a time.

I began to lean more heavily on others than I ever had in my life. I got really sick of being alone and learned the value of asking for help (and graciously accepting it even when I didn't ask). New friends became close friends very quickly. My ex-husband, his wife, and his mother brought me into their family and took care of me on more than one occasion when I needed family and none of mine were available. I was blessed by the people in my life and I realized that more and more every day. John trusted that I'd be taken care of by them and they were doing a great job.

I was making big changes quickly, which is something the experts say you're not supposed to do. But those changes felt right for me. Honestly, I still felt like John was helping me make these decisions, like we were making them together in a way because we had talked at length about what would be best for me once he was gone. He had told me he wanted me to move back to the Pacific Northwest where I had good friends and most of my family close by. We had talked about moving back there together before his disease progressed to the point where we knew he was terminal.

What I hadn't anticipated before John died was how painful it would be to stay in Walla Walla, where all of our memories were, or live in the house where he died once he was gone. I decided not to wait to relocate. I felt like I was making this move for both of us. I sold my home in Walla Walla, saying goodbye to the happy memories (and also many of the painful ones), and bought a brand new home in Vancouver, Washington, close to Portland, Oregon and most of my family.

It all definitely felt like progress, like I was coming to the edge of the heavy, deep, dark forest of grief through which I'd been trekking. I also know that I did so much grieving in the months before John died that I might have gotten a head start. I know it allowed me to actually grieve with him, crying on his shoulder every night when we went to bed, asking him how I'd possibly live without him, and hearing him say how sorry he was that he didn't have an answer for me.

Most importantly, I knew that happiness was what John wanted for me. I knew he was proud of me. All he ever wanted when he was alive was for me to be happy. That didn't change once he was gone. I was becoming a little happier every day.

During that busy time of so much change, I also became keenly aware that I was often holding both joy, and feelings of optimism and eager anticipation, right alongside feelings of sorrow and grief. It was something I had never experienced before. I realized that I could allow joy back in, while still actively grieving all of the loss I was also experiencing.

In that space, with both palms turned up—willing to receive whatever came—I realized that joy and sorrow are not that far apart on my emotional scale. I had cried lots of tears in the past nine months or so, once we learned John was terminal and certainly after he died, and after a while, some of those became tears of joy. I was in a constant state of reaching out and grabbing hold of the new life I was creating for myself while I struggled to let go of what had come before. I was buying the house of my dreams back "home" where my family and friends lived and in order to have that, I had to let go of my house in Walla Walla and the friends who had been my family there.

I staged my current house and packed away every scrap of personalization that was in it. Every photo, every saved love note tacked on my bulletin board from John, every memento from my life over the past decade. It felt like I was packing away that life and it was exhausting and sad. I had lived in that house for twelve years. I'd bought it as a single mom. My boys had grown up in that house. I met John and he moved in with me in that house. We made an incredible life together there, and it was where he had exited my life after the most difficult two and a half years I'd ever experienced. So there was much joy there but also too much pain for me to stay.

While it was very hard to leave, it was necessary if I wanted to move forward and into my new life. And yet again, it left me wanting to hold on while needing to let go, feeling joy in the midst of my continuing sorrow.

CHAPTER 11

MOVING FORWARD

About four months after he died, I memorialized John's Facebook account and changed my status to widowed. That was a tough milestone but a necessary step for me.

I was in a strange place of wanting to hold on to (even live in, if I was being honest) the past, and knowing that I needed to move forward and step into my new life and my new self. For a long time I didn't think I'd ever feel joy again. Then, almost overnight, I started grabbing it with both hands with every chance I got. I've never been a sipper. I've always gulped, taken big steps, and walked fast. That's what I was doing, after moving in slow motion and wondering if I'd ever feel like myself again. I knew I'd never be the same but I also realized that I was becoming someone wiser, stronger, and more grateful because of my loss. Astoundingly, the worst thing to ever happen to me was also impacting who I was in a hugely positive way.

I started dating again, slowly dipping my toe back into the "love" pool. This was something my sweet, wise Johnny told me would happen. "You're a partnership person," he said to me a few weeks before he died. "You need a partner and I want you to have that." He also told me that I'd probably "partner" sooner than anyone thought appropriate. "Do it anyhow," he said. Then, with that familiar twinkle in his eye, he smiled and said, "I'll send you the perfect person."

He was right about people not approving of me dating "so soon" after he died. I remember one of my friends at the time overhearing a conversation about how inappropriate it was that I was dating (between two people who were still happily living with their very alive husbands). She said to them, "You realize her husband is dead, right? How long do you think she should wait? Who gets to decide what's an appropriate amount of time? Is there a book of rules somewhere she's somehow missing?"

I began to feel like I'd survived the worst of the brutal grief process. I certainly knew I was not out of the woods by any means, but there was more happiness and joy in my days than sorrow, so that was huge progress. Through that transition, I could feel John with me, cheering me on and—as he always had when he was alive—wanting the best for me.

I was deliberately choosing joy whenever possible and moving forward even when it felt damn scary. Those choices were the best way I could imagine to keep John's legacy (of living life to its fullest and always finding the positive in every situation) alive.

The July after John died, I packed up the last of my stuff in my Walla Walla house. The next day, as I drove away, I remember praying that I would never have to come back. Now, more than ever, I needed to put that house and that part of my life behind me in order to move forward.

The night before my final trip back to Walla Walla to tie up loose ends and finalize my move, I sat on my bed in my big new master bedroom in my dream house and a heaviness began to settle over me. I realized that the house in Walla Walla, where John and I had shared our entire lives together, had been energetically draining me since the moment he died. It wasn't just the memories and sadness surrounding that time or the haunting memories of him crying the day before he died (skeletal and barely recognizable, half unconscious, and telling us he was sad because he didn't want to go but knew he had to). That was huge, for sure, but I realized there was more to it than that.

The house itself was energetically sad. I had spent most of the previous two months away from there, deliberately making myself busy with things to do in Portland. Every time I drove back to Walla Walla, the sadness would creep back in, little by little, as I drove east up the Columbia Gorge. I dreaded walking into the house, living and working and sleeping there. It was permeated with such a huge amount of sadness that it was overwhelming. I had adjusted to it over the six months since I'd lost John and I don't think I really even realized how powerful it was until I moved out and moved on.

From the moment I set foot in my new house, I felt myself slowly but deliberately coming back to myself. I felt grounded and stronger than I'd felt in months. Strong for myself, not for John or my kids. I felt more capable than ever of standing on my own two feet and being happy on my own.

Moving into the new house was liberating. It was like I could finally unpack the sweet, wonderful memories of John as I was unpacking my dishes and pots and pans. It was refreshing to be able to think about him and our life together for the six years we had before the brutal final six months of his life. And I felt such relief and happiness at those memories. They weren't tinged with sadness like they always had been living in Walla Walla.

I moved all of the good things I remembered about our life together with me and I knew energetically he'd come too, that his positive energy, the best part of him, would always be with me.

Right after I moved in, I was texting with a new friend (one who hadn't known me before that month) about life's struggles and challenges. Her daughter (and only child) was heading off to college that month and she was facing lots of changes in her life. I shared the second part of the THRIVE process with her (Honor your feelings) and told her the best advice I got when John died was to "feel all the feels" and lean into them, even if it was painful. She said my story inspired her and (since I hadn't yet), I sent her the link to the blog. I told her to start at the beginning if she wanted to read our whole story. She thanked me and said she needed some inspiration.

I responded, "It's an inspiring story but spoiler alert... the hero dies in the end." I was attempting to be glib, but as I stepped into the shower after sending that text, the floodgates opened and I had what they called in my grief support group, a "grief storm." Even now, many years later, I still have them occasionally. They are like a hurricane when they come, blowing through my day, out of control and yet controlling me. They only last a little while and then they're gone—but just like a hurricane, often the devastation they leave behind takes me some time to clean up.

During the months after John died, when I'd be hit with that type of grief and I cried, I didn't recognize the sound. It was a wailing, keening, utterly painful cry that came from somewhere inside me I'd never tapped into before losing him. The first time I heard myself cry that way was about five minutes after John took his last breath. I sat on the stairs holding his daughter Chelsey, trying to comfort her through my own unbearable grief, and finally letting go of all I'd been holding on to for so many months as we fought through the end of John's life. It all came out in huge, loud, messy, uncontrollable sobs that lasted about ten minutes. I remember being truly amazed at the sound of it—so unfamiliar and anguished—that it caught me off guard.

That week in September, I cried because I was finally there, in my new home, settling in alone. I cried because the sale of my Walla Walla home had come through and that stressful time was finally over—along with that part of my life. It was a bittersweet realization. I cried because I didn't want to spend the rest of my life alone but I also knew that I wouldn't settle in order to NOT be alone.

But mostly, I cried because I missed my husband and best friend. So much, every single day. Even in a new place with no actual "memories" of him tied to my house or surroundings other than the pictures I was hanging, I still just missed him, and the way I felt when I was with him. Finding someone who accepts you for who you are (in fact, loves you because of it and not in spite of it) and who makes your life sweet and fun and happy, just by being in it, is a huge gift.

I love this quote…

> "I wanted a perfect ending. Now I've learned, the hard way, that some poems don't rhyme, and some stories don't have a clear beginning, middle, and end. Life is about not knowing, having to change, taking the moment and making the best of it, without knowing what's going to happen next. Delicious Ambiguity." ~Gilda Radner

I had no idea how very true this quote would be for me. I was discovering that life did go on and every day it got easier to breathe and laugh and plan for the future. Some days the ambiguity of my current life actually DID feel delicious, even spacious. Other days I couldn't help but wistfully think back to the plan I *thought* I had for my life, with a beautiful man who wasn't perfect but was perfect for me, who loved me more than I loved myself most of the time, who had my back always, and whom I was supposed to laugh and love with until we both grew old and gray.

On those days, I still felt robbed.

So much had changed for me since John had died. There had been times I hadn't known how I would survive one more day. I never wallowed in self pity or felt sorry for myself, but I also didn't fight the sadness when it hit. I learned early on that it's futile to do that and I knew it was part of my healing process. I leaned into it, let myself feel everything, and then blew my nose and moved on.

I was strong most days and weak once in a while. I didn't argue with what I was feeling or even try to understand why I was feeling it. It didn't really matter. Grief is a challenging journey—and a difficult one to navigate. One minute it's a beautiful, sunny drive on a straight road through scenery you love looking at—and the next, it's sharp, steep curves that sneak up on you and force you to hit the brakes and hold on for dear life.

The one thing I've learned about this journey is that I have to keep driving. There's no turning around and going back. But on the particularly hard days, when I was pulled to remember so much from our past, I found myself wishing that u-turns were permitted and that I could go back.

CHAPTER 12

HAVING MY OWN BACK

About a month after John died, as I cried on her shoulder for the millionth time, a good friend told me to hang on. She promised me that I wouldn't feel this way forever, that the pain would begin to fade and my life would come back to center. She told me I'd feel better again someday and I just needed to hold on through this part. She promised me that, once I had a year under my belt, my whole world would look different.

She told me to just hold on, that this would pass. To give it a year.

A year, at that point, felt like a lifetime to me. Hell, a day felt like a lifetime, like something I might not make it through. It was hard to believe in her promise because I was in such intense, almost-unbearable pain and I couldn't see my way out of it. It felt like the darkness would never lift.

2016 was a long, brutally painful year of huge changes. I was not sorry to see it end.

As I approached the final day of that year, the one thing I could proclaim (loudly and with conviction), was that I HAD survived. In fact, I was actually thriving in some areas.

It had been a very long road. I had cried an ocean of tears, but I wasn't crying every day anymore. Sometimes I even went for several days without crying. I had battled depression for the first time in my life, and fought my way out of it to find joy again.

I'd learned a few things as well. I'd learned I was stronger than I ever thought I could be. I'm a happy person by nature and that happiness was firmly in place in my life again. I'm an action-taker and action had restored my life during that difficult year. I sold my house, bought a house, moved 250 miles, dealt with everything that huge move entailed, and was settled and happy in my new home and town.

I was a different person than I had been a year ago. I was wiser and more present. I could go a few days without checking my email. That was something I'd NEVER done in the past. I'd learned to define very carefully what was really important in my life and to focus my attention on that.

I was able to let things go more easily and didn't sweat nearly as much small stuff as I had before.

Most importantly, I'd learned to love and trust myself, to love my body, love who I was, and to have my own back for the first time in my life. I didn't need anyone else's love or approval to be ok with who I was. I knew I could do that for myself. I surprised myself a few times with that newfound confidence, but I felt like it was the greatest gift I'd taken away from my mourning experience.

Life looked amazing from where I was sitting now. Even looking back at the past year, with all the pain and growth, I felt good about where I was and what my future looked like. I had reinvented myself (because I had to, not because I wanted to) and I was thrilled about who I'd become and what the changes I'd embraced meant for my future.

I still had tough days now and then, but the good days far outnumbered the bad ones. And even on bad days, I could look at the good in my life and the people who loved me and be grateful for it all. I was focused on happiness and on letting my life unfold beautifully and naturally, fine with not knowing what was coming for the first time in a very long time. I was content with reading the book of my life instead of writing it. It was a huge change for me but a good and necessary one.

For the past year I couldn't make a plan because grief was running the show. At the start of that year, I was content with not having a plan because I had learned that I didn't need to control anything except focusing on feeling good. When I did that, everything unfolded beautifully and things worked out in my favor. I was trusting The Universe and excited to see where my life would take me.

CHAPTER 13

LOVE WINS

About a year into John's cancer battle, after I'd been writing the blog consistently and people started saying I should turn it into a book, I remember my standard answer was that I would write the book once I had my happy ending. At that time, the only happy ending I could imagine was John beating cancer and us living happily ever after. When he died, I honestly thought, if I did write the book the best I could hope for was an ending where I'd come to grips with losing him and was managing to survive without him. I guess I thought I would re-partner but I never thought I'd find a love like I had with John again. We had an incredible love and the odds of having anything even close to that again were pretty small. Or so I thought.

John had other plans—and he never had any doubt that I'd find happiness like we had again. He told me before he died that he'd send me the perfect person. Leave it to him to make good on that promise. In April 2017, I met the next great love of my life.

I met Mark Kick at the perfect time—when I was finally ready. From the moment we met, it was clear to me that he was my person. Not only does he love me for exactly who I am, but he's completely sensitive to my ongoing grief journey and has never, ever felt threatened by the "other" man in my life.

When we first met, one of the things I told Mark was if we moved forward, there would be three people in our relationship and that he'd have to "get to know" John, because he was still such a huge part of my life. He has never had a problem with that. He laughs at my stories and holds on to me when the grief storms hit. Mark says he worries that he could never fill the hole John left. I agree with him. Nothing will ever fill that void. But he opened up beautiful new spaces in my heart, and helped me to see a path through the rest of my life that was filled with love and laughter and happiness.

That's all John ever wanted for me while he was alive and even after he died. I think he's smiling down today, proud of where I am and happy that I'm happy. It raises the question… how can I be so much in love with Mark and still miss my husband to the point of tears sometimes? Grief is weird and sticky and frustrating.

Sometimes I wonder what I did to deserve Mark, but I know the answer. I've survived more since John died than I ever thought I would in a lifetime. I've kept going even when I didn't think I could take another step or live another day. I've allowed myself to feel every sucky feeling, and every bit of joy, and I've never lost hope that life could be amazing and beautiful again. As I've moved forward from John's death and found the second great love of my life in Mark, I've come to understand that I'm in love with two men at the same time.

I'll never stop loving John. I hold him in my heart and mind, there are pictures of him all over our home, and much of who I am now is because of how he loved me. I'm extremely lucky to have found a man in Mark who is completely okay with me maintaining that love for my late husband. He's never been threatened or offended by it. I cry in his arms over John sometimes and I think it's astounding that he can hold me, allow me to have that grief storm, and often even cries with me. That's been a huge gift to me. He also loves my stepchildren and has become "grandpa" to my stepdaughter's daughter. We have built an unlikely and beautiful family and I am extremely grateful.

Do I still grieve this huge, tragic loss? Without a doubt. Do I still miss John? Every single day. But I'm moving on with intention and passion, and building a new life—in part because that's exactly what he expected, demanded even, that I do. I will always be grateful for the short time we had and all that he taught me. John gave me the gift of myself and taught me how to be loved. I will never stop missing him.

Mark and I married on August 3rd, 2019, with John's kids, my kids, and Mark's son standing beside us. In my vows to him I said, "I won't say I believe in happily ever after anymore (because I have a very acute understanding of how fragile life is and how precious every moment), but I do know that what I'm feeling now is something I honestly never thought I'd feel again. Optimistic about a future spent with someone who gets me better than anyone alive (since John was the only other person who fell into that category), loves me unconditionally, and with whom I can see myself building a future and growing old."

Just like I said on the day John died, in the end, love wins. Cancer loses and love wins.

PART 3

THE THRIVE
PROCESS

CHAPTER 14

YOU TOO CAN THRIVE AGAIN

During the final week of John's life, I wrote a post on our Love Trumps Cancer blog that went viral. It was shared several thousand times and read by thousands of people. I remember sharing that with him and wondering aloud if the impact his story was making was somehow the reason for his death (and life). We talked about the fact that, if any good could come from his death, that would be it. It didn't really help me at the time, but it made some sense.

I had a large following for my speaking and training business before I began sharing our story through the blog, and over the course of writing it, thousands of people reached out (either privately or via comments on my Facebook posts) and shared that our story had impacted them profoundly. That was gratifying for both of us. It helped me to process my feelings by writing them out (since I've been a writer my whole life). More than that, however—and a byproduct of sharing such an intimate journey so honestly—was the support I got from this large community of people who, for the most part, I had never met and didn't know outside of social media. I learned to lean on others when it felt like I couldn't go on.

I also came to understand that I could endure the unimaginable and still find happiness again. The two and a half years while John was sick and dying were extremely difficult, and surviving after his death was unimaginably, brutally hard. But I did survive. In fact, after about a year, I was honestly thriving. That had been his goal for me. John knew how strong I was and he never doubted that strength—even when I did. The interesting thing about my own THRIVE journey, as I look back, is that the only way I could truly begin to thrive again was to feel the pain and honor my feelings every step of the way. It required holding both joy and pain in the same space. I still do that quite often.

It was out of this shift that the THRIVE Process evolved. Once I had the time, distance, and personal growth to rise above my story and see how I moved through it, the parts of this process emerged. Now that you know my story, I want to share the exact steps of the THRIVE process and how I used it to navigate this most difficult season of my life. I still use parts of it daily. It's my hope that you'll be better able to understand this process by viewing it through the lens of my story so that you can more easily apply it to yours.

CHAPTER 15

TRUST YOURSELF

The first letter in the THRIVE process
stands for Trust Yourself.

This is first for a reason. When you're dealing with a huge loss of any kind, it throws your world into a tailspin. And when the world is falling to pieces around you, and you don't feel like you can trust anything, being able to tap into your intuition, higher power, or whatever you call it, is crucial. I believe that my intuition is my higher power speaking directly to me. Often, what I hear from that source totally surprises me, challenges me, and asks me to step outside of my comfort zone. I can also honestly say that trusting that voice has never let me down.

Growing up female in the 1970s and 80s, I was definitely predisposed to please others and I started seeking the approval of my parents, teachers, and really anyone in a position of authority from an early age. Even pleasing the adults in my life, however, took a backseat to fitting in at all costs—which meant allowing my peers to dictate what I should and shouldn't do. I constantly worried about how I looked all through growing up and into my early twenties. I also worried about what I said and did, and what other people saw when they looked at me. It took me years to move away from the outside influences that asked me to conform, and to embrace the late Wayne Dyer's assertion that, "what other people think of you is none of your business." I'm still not completely there, but as I approach my sixties, I'm close.

Moving from trusting outside sources to trusting yourself is a process that can take time, and it's obviously different for everyone. I promise you, doing the work to hear and to actually start listening to your intuition is worth the investment. It doesn't mean you'll never seek trusted counsel from others, but even the people you listen to can change when you start trusting yourself. The first thing I noticed when I really started to embrace my own guidance was that the people whose opinions and advice had previously mattered to me greatly, suddenly just didn't. I learned that the people who were worth listening to were mostly telling me to trust myself. They were asking questions instead of giving advice. And when I did ask them for advice, they were basically still telling me to look inside for those answers.

While John was going through all of the treatments and surgeries that marked his cancer journey, I trusted myself and listened to my intuition over and over again. I learned that doctors don't always have all the answers and that no doctor had my husband's best interest at heart as much as I did. Sometimes I had to learn to push back if something didn't seem right—like basically demanding that they put the feeding tube in, something that probably prolonged John's life by at least two weeks. That follow-the-rules girl from the '70s didn't like it when I questioned authority, but my intuition made it clear that what she thought wasn't important.

If you've sustained a great loss, whether it's the death of someone you love, a divorce, or any other huge life event, you're already on shaky ground. You'll find fairly quickly that well-meaning people who probably actually do love you, feel more obligated during these times than at any other to swoop in and "fix" your life. There are more people telling you what you should and shouldn't do during times of crisis than at any other time in your life. So, even if you generally trust yourself most of the time, it's more difficult after a huge loss, when you can find yourself literally feeling lost. Add to that the fact that there is a subset of rules—written or just implied—of which you may suddenly find yourself being reminded. You're supposed to act a certain way, grieve a certain way, wait a respectable amount of time to restart your life or get back to normal (whatever that means). It's accepted wisdom that you're not supposed to make any big life changes for at least a year after you suffer a great loss, since decisions made while you're grieving may not ultimately be in your best interest.

I read those books and I heard that advice. I ignored most of it because my intuition was telling me that staying where I was would be too painful to allow me to begin healing. Choosing to sell the home I'd shared with John and move back to the area where I'd grown up and had family was the best choice I could make. It went against the standard wisdom, but my intuition was screaming that it was the right thing for me. I will never regret making that move.

I can pinpoint the day my healing started right down to the first night I spent in my new home. If I'd followed other's advice during that time (including the "experts" and my counselor), it would have delayed the forward motion that was created by that move. In my case, I'd had the luxury of discussing my next moves with my husband before he died and we both agreed that moving would be best. But it was still a big leap of faith for me, and was driven by me knowing what was best for me. That came from trusting myself.

There is no specific law around how soon a widow should start dating again, but there is judgement to spare if you start "too soon." I started dating again after about six months. Too soon? Believe me, I heard that, either directly from people who felt like they knew what was best for me, or third-party from close friends who had been approached by "concerned" mutual friends. John and I had discussed my re-partnering. He was for it, and I couldn't imagine it—until a few months after he died, as the loneliness set in, and it started to look like something I might want to explore. Without those first few initial dating experiences, I wouldn't have recognized Mark when he came along.

Dipping my toe back into the dating pool felt right. That's the point. What other people thought of my decisions was none of my business. It only mattered what I thought was best for me, and that started with trusting myself. So ask yourself, what feels right for you? If the answer is a bit unorthodox or bucks the norm (unless it's something that will actually harm you), that's okay. It's what's right for you. Keep checking in with yourself. If it feels wrong, listen to that voice just as much and do something different.

There's one other thing losing John taught me about trusting myself. It's the true, deep understanding that life is short. My life (and yours too, by the way), can change in the blink of an eye, in the beat of a heart, with a phone call from a doctor or a visit from a police officer. Tomorrow is not guaranteed for any of us. Today is truly all we have. And as I started contemplating making changes and moving on without John, I knew I had no intention of waiting for one single day to live my life to its fullest.

Why would I wait to fall in love again? My husband was gone and—if there was one thing I'd come to accept during the months after he died (even though it took a little time)—it was that he was never, ever coming back. I could wait ten days or ten years to start dating again and that fact was never changing. He wanted me to move on, to be happy, to live my life and love again. He didn't expect me to wait a "respectable" amount of time to do that. Living full out honors our love and his legacy. And that starts with truly listening to myself and trusting what I hear.

I'd love to tell you that I have a clear process for tapping into my intuition, but I really don't. I'm not good at meditation and after fighting with myself for years, I finally decided that it wasn't for me. I don't pray in the traditional sense of the word either. I do write my feelings very well, and that has certainly been my go-to process as much as anything has. I also employ affirmations and I believe in, and use, visualization to activate the Law of Attraction. I did all those things after John died.

The point is, both meditation and prayer can certainly lead you to tap into your own answers and start trusting yourself, just like journaling or visualization can. Whatever gets you to stop, ask, get quiet, and listen is what you should do. It's also really important to allow your intuition to access you at unexpected times and to listen then as well. I often get intuitive nudges when I'm in the shower or driving. Stay open, learn to listen, and trust yourself.

CHAPTER 16

HONOR
YOUR FEELINGS

The H in the THRIVE process
stands for Honor Your Feelings.

After John died, the most consistent piece of advice I got was to "feel all the feelings." Even though I haven't always been able to lean in when emotions strike (especially to negative emotion), this was probably the easiest part of the process for me to master. That's not to say it was easy at all to feel those feelings, but I found that giving myself permission to do so was easier after losing John—especially at the very beginning of the grieving process. It was almost as if, for the first time in my life, I had permission to just feel. Nobody expected me to hide my pain.

I honestly made it my job to lean in to every sucky feeling, get through it, and move on. And the fact that this level of grief was a brand new experience for me honestly gave me permission, since I had no idea what to expect. That's important. It's wise to fully experience any emotions you're having (and know that it's always ok to do so whether you're grieving or just going through usual life things), but for me, it took deep, intense grief to really understand and embrace that concept. That's because—unlike any other time in my life—the intense emotions I experienced (especially at the end of John's life and for several months after he died), were beyond anything I'd ever known before and they would not be ignored. I pretty much had no choice.

It taught me to stop—no matter where I was—and feel the feeling. Sometimes that wasn't convenient. Often it happened during times or in places that weren't private. A few times it made those around me uncomfortable—because we humans aren't really sure what to do with our own powerful emotions, let alone someone else's—which made me uncomfortable. But grief doesn't care about any of that and I realized very quickly at the beginning of my grief journey that to ignore an emotion, while it might work in the short term, meant it would come back around again—usually stronger and more insistent than ever. As I said earlier in this book, ignoring a strong emotion is like endlessly driving around and around a busy traffic circle, too afraid to merge to the right. Eventually, you have to take your exit and move on. It's hard and sometimes scary, but necessary.

So know that it's okay to feel every emotion—no matter what it is—fully and completely and in any way you need to. If that means pulling over to the side of the road and pounding your steering wheel and screaming until you're hoarse when an emotion hits, do it. If it means watching a comedy and laughing until you wet your pants, do that too. I promise, there's no wrong emotion and no wrong way to express it.

It's expected that you'll experience strong emotion right after a devastating loss. What's less expected (but no less intense) is the emotion fueled by years-old grief. At this writing, it's been over five years since John died and I still have moments occasionally that stop me cold, take the air out of my lungs, and bring me to my knees. They are never expected and always powerful. For me, these grief storms have been more difficult to accept and have patience with than the melt downs I had in the middle of public places weeks after John died—especially the further away from his death I get. "It's been a long time," my logical mind tells me, "You shouldn't be crying over this." It doesn't happen very often—and it almost always comes out of the blue—when a sight or a sound catches me off guard and I feel gutted all of a sudden, devastated all over again at the loss of my beloved. But it still happens and I'm convinced it will until the day I die.

As the years have passed and I've come to realize that these unexpected visits from grief will never go away, I'm learning to deal with them. I think it's even harder for me because I've always been basically a no-excuses, pragmatic person—never prone to dramatic outbursts or anxiety attacks. I honestly never really had much patience for those who experienced those things. Now I do.

The first time I was in a hospital after John died was for a simple outpatient surgery. It had been about eight months since his last hospital stay. Everything was fine. I changed into the surgery gown and laid down on the bed to wait for the nurse. As I stared up at the ceiling something—I'm still not sure what—triggered a grief storm that bordered on an anxiety attack and, out of nowhere, the tears started to flow. I couldn't control them and had to explain to the nurse what was happening. I've had three outpatient surgeries in the years since and have had the exact same experience each time. It's disconcerting but I take my own advice, honor the feelings I'm having, and move on.

I encourage you to find spaces and people where you can safely access your emotions, especially your pain. That will mean different things for everyone, but using a counselor or support group where you feel comfortable and have support no matter how you're feeling or expressing emotion, can be life saving—especially in the very beginning of your grieving process, when your emotions will be at their most intense. Even a trusted friend who knows you and whom you trust can be a huge help.

CHAPTER 17

REMAIN PRESENT

The R in the THRIVE process
stands for Remain Present.

This represents the opportunity to remain present as the literal story of your grief unfolds. As with every step in this process, there's a level of acceptance and of embracing everything that's happening to you—whether you label it as good or bad—during this step. What do I mean by remain present? I mean accept where you are now, today, knowing that things will inevitably change tomorrow. Accept it even if it's painful. Just having the ability to accept your current reality can provide a level of perspective that helps you get through today. You may have to remind yourself to be present twenty times a day, but for that brief instant when you are able to do it, you'll feel some relief.

Since I blogged throughout John's cancer journey and for a few years after his death, my story unfolded gradually over time. I shared my current reality with honesty and transparency. Nothing was sugar coated, because I wanted to be as present to everything as I possibly could. I would often go back and re-read blog posts I'd written in the past, or catch a Facebook memory that popped up to remind me of how my story had changed. I still do. It may seem morbid, but it's important to me to see where I was and how far I've come. I'm also very grateful that I had the blog—written as I was present to and experiencing the things I wrote about—to draw on as I wrote this book. Had I relied on my memory of those events, this would have been a different book, because perspective and time changes your perception of events.

The important thing to remember is that the need to be present to your own experience and emotions isn't unique to people who are grieving, it's just more obvious and a lot more painful. Evolution is part of the human experience. Your life story starts unfolding from the moment you enter the world and doesn't stop until you exit it. It changes whether or not you experience a devastating loss. The fact that this part of your story may be extremely painful and difficult to write doesn't make it any less a part of your story. You may wish it weren't happening or want it to be different, and that's natural. But you still have to own your journey, even when it's very difficult. For me, having the ability to share what was happening through the written word made a huge, positive difference in how I experienced it. As I've said, writing is cathartic for me.

If you're not a writer, find a different way to express yourself. Maybe it's through music or just talking it out with someone you trust. When you force yourself to sit in a room with your emotions, you gain power over them. The other thing staying present does is actually allow you to progress through—and eventually beyond—the most intense part of your grief. As with the other two steps we've covered so far, the more access you gain to your emotions, the more readily you can move forward. As you start to feel better and your life starts to shift into a new reality devoid of the person or thing that you've lost, you can begin to chart a new path toward joy again. You'll start to find a new normal. It takes time and, if your loss is very fresh, you may feel like it will never happen, but the more present you can be with what's happening now, the easier it will be to embrace what's going to happen next. And you'll walk into it with the perspective of what you've learned from your journey up until now, including the grief part of it.

Sometimes this happens gradually and you wake up one day and realize you haven't cried a single tear in over a week. Sometimes, it hits you like a flash, as you laugh with a friend and find yourself feeling genuinely good for the first time in recent memory. It's tempting (and natural) to feel guilty the first time that happens after a loss—as if you're somehow disrespecting the sorrow your lost loved one so richly deserves from you. It's almost as if you've been caught doing something you're not supposed to do. I remember wanting to post something light hearted or funny on social media a few weeks after John died and thinking, "What will people think if I do that? I'm supposed to be grieving." Then I realized that to NOT allow myself to feel joy again was not only damaging me, but dishonoring John's memory and legacy. And I could practically hear him whispering into my ear, "Stop it! You're supposed to be happy!"

As I've said in earlier chapters, I was amazed when I realized that I could hold both joy and sorrow in the same space at the same time. I also realized that in order to truly move through the grief and continue with my life, I'd have to learn to do that. Some days I still do. When John's daughter Chelsey had her baby, almost five years after John died, my first reaction was deep sorrow and the most intense longing for him that I'd felt in many years. I literally burst into tears, and they weren't initially happy tears. They came from my sorrow for all that he was missing. He would have been so thrilled and made an absolutely amazing grandpa. Then I laughed through my tears and embraced my beautiful new granddaughter, feeling intense joy at the privilege of being in her life. Joy and sorrow, in the same instant. I'm grateful I was able to be present to both emotions, and for the understanding—which was made more poignant because of what I've lost—of just how amazing life really is.

CHAPTER 18

INVEST IN YOURSELF

The I in the THRIVE process
stands for Invest in Yourself.

Investing in yourself isn't necessarily about making a financial investment. For our purposes, it's paying attention to what you need and being willing to make the investment of time and energy in order to get it—either from yourself or by asking for help from others. Especially if you've been a caregiver for any length of time prior to your loss, this is much easier said than done. Your default is probably to take care of everyone but yourself. And asking for help may not be something you've ever done, or at least not something that's ever come easily for you.

At the end of John's life, as his health was rapidly spiraling downward, I had to force myself to ask for and accept help from others. It wasn't comfortable for me. It made me feel like I wasn't up to the job of taking care of him and I was really hard on myself. Over the two and a half years during which John was sick, I was pretty much his sole caregiver. That wasn't necessarily because I was the only one who could do it, it was just expected. And everybody else in our lives had their own lives. When you're not faced with the hard reality of how difficult cancer treatment is on a daily basis, it's easy to assume the person going through it is fine. John presented an "I'm fine" face to the world for most of his illness, no matter how sick he really was. So people probably didn't think he needed as much care as I was giving him. And I was too proud to ask for help.

When he went on hospice, he needed full-time care that was much more involved. He had a feeding tube and that was a huge learning curve. He was getting daily fluids to help him keep his strength up and we had a home health nurse come and show me how to administer those through his port. I am not a nurse and the whole medical aspect of John's care, especially at the end of his life, was extremely stressful for me. When he reached the point, about a week before he died, that he needed middle of the night care in addition to the care he required during the day, I broke.

Turning over responsibility for his care to his brother and kids was one of the hardest things I had to do during that last week. I wanted to be the one meeting all of his needs but it just wasn't physically possible. I was exhausted and emotionally drained. So, for the first time in years, I did what was best for me. I asked for help even though it was the last thing I wanted to do. It's something you'll have to learn to do too, and it's definitely part of investing in yourself. Others want to support you but they don't know what you need or how to help. It's up to you to ask.

After John died, this was even more difficult. As I shared in part two of this book, once the memorial service was over and everyone went back to their own lives, I was no longer top of mind for them. I don't blame anyone for that, but it was my reality. I had to either reach out and say, "I'm lonely and I need to hang out," or, "Can I come for dinner?" or I would spend all of my time alone. I did a fair job of asking for support, but not as good as I could have. I spent too much time alone and it wasn't good for me. Since I'm an extrovert, part of the way I process is to literally talk it out. So I needed people around me in order to be able to do that. You might not. In fact, asking for help for you may look like telling people you need space. Either way, you are the only one who will know what you need. You cannot expect people to read your mind. You are responsible for knowing and asking for what you need.

The beauty of doing that (especially at the beginning of your grief journey when it's the most intense), is that, in my experience and more than at any other time in my life, people gave me maximum grace. It's okay for you to say, "Come help me," one day and, "leave me alone," the next. Everybody will understand that what you need on any given day will change and that's okay. Take full advantage of that grace and ask for what you need.

Time is another huge investment that's required at this step in the THRIVE process. You must give yourself the time and space to grieve, no matter what that looks like. As I said in an earlier chapter, you can't know how any day will unfold for you, especially in the beginning of your grieving journey. It's important that you continually check in with yourself and allow things to unfold naturally. It takes patience and being present. Truthfully, whether or not you are actually present to this part of the process, it will unfold. Grief demands your time and attention and, like a screaming infant or a persistent pet, it will not be ignored.

I'm a planner and am hyper organized and those traits have always helped me deal with big changes in my life. So I assumed making a plan and sticking to it would get me through losing my husband as well. There were days during those first few months when I had a great plan to create a training program, or work on a marketing piece for my business and, when the time came to actually put pen to paper, there was just no way it was happening. Because grief had other plans for that day. I learned quickly that there was nothing I could do but ride the wave. It was frustrating when I fought it, but when I just made the time and space and leaned in, I was generally able to get through it more quickly and get back to whatever plan I'd had to abandon.

Investing in yourself means constantly evaluating your energy and your physical and mental state, and being willing to take care of yourself based on what you need. You may not feel like eating, but eating is essential for you to maintain your health. So invest in eating healthily. You may not feel like getting out of bed to work out, but physical activity will help your mindset and your physical body, so make yourself get up and do something, even if it's just taking a walk around the block. Self-care is always an important investment, no matter what's happening in your life, but when you're actively grieving, it's even more important. So invest in self-care above all else.

Finally, regardless of how you feel about talking about your feelings, counseling of some sort is an investment you must make. Trusting a professional who specializes in grief made a huge difference for me. Since John was on hospice when he died, I was eligible for their grief counseling services at no charge. When they first contacted me, I was reluctant, only because my loss was so fresh and I was just barely surviving each day. I could not entertain the thought of doing anything to help me move forward, because I wasn't ready. About six weeks out from losing John, however, I did say yes (and huge props to the hospice counselor who kept following up with me until I was ready).

I only had three sessions with my counselor—and then I moved on to a grief support group that she facilitated—but those sessions literally saved me. All she did was grief counseling so she knew exactly what I needed to hear, and how I needed to hear it. She gave me permission to feel whatever I was feeling, and more importantly, she shared a completely different perspective with me about some of the things I was thinking and feeling that changed the way I looked at them. I am eternally grateful for her help, and to myself for saying yes to it. Even if it's not offered to you for free, I highly recommend that you seek out a counselor who specializes in your type of grief and make the investment in yourself. It doesn't have to take months. Even a few sessions can make an enormous difference.

CHAPTER 19

VOW TO ACT

The V in the THRIVE process
stands for Vow to Act.

This step in the process will happen later in your grief journey. Honestly, at the beginning, any action you take at all is difficult and often not intentional. Days pass by and nothing really gets done because you don't have much capacity to do them. Even if you are taking care of children or going to work, chances are good you're just going through the motions and in survival mode. And that's on your best days.

The action I'm referring to with this step is intentional, transitional action. It's forward movement toward something, even if it's not specific. For me, that meant making a plan to move from Walla Walla in eastern Washington State to Vancouver, in the southwestern part of the state and just across the border from Portland, Oregon, where my family lived and where I'd grown up. I didn't know exactly how that action would unfold, but I knew where I wanted to be. Initially, I considered keeping my home in Walla Walla and either renting it out or turning it into a vacation rental and then renting a home in Vancouver. I even looked at a few rental houses there. In the end, it was easier to sell my home and buy something in my new city. I had what I thought was a fixed budget as I started shopping for homes, and then found a brand new, under construction house that was $100,000.00 over my budget that I intuitively knew I was supposed to buy. And so I did.

The point is, I didn't know what the move was going to look like or how it was going to unfold, but I vowed that I was going to move. Just the act of making that commitment set the ball in motion and everything unfolded from there. I took a huge leap and it was a big transition. I had to pack up and sell my home in Walla Walla, go through the stress of financing a new home as a self employed person, and uproot my entire life to move 250 miles from the place I'd lived for almost twenty years. You don't have to do anything as dramatic.

Take baby steps or take a huge leap. It really doesn't matter, as long as you make a commitment and vow to act. You'll find that a series of tiny steps can eventually lead to a big leap. Declaring that you'll do anything in and of itself has power. You don't have to take immediate action once you make that commitment, and in actuality, just choosing something you want and focusing on having it will activate the Law of Attraction and things will begin to unfold for you. But it begins with that vow to act, to move forward in some way.

This won't necessarily be easy. Transition is difficult in the best of circumstances, and can be very challenging when you're in the middle of grieving a loss. The thing to understand is that it's ok if it's hard, and it's ok if it takes time. You don't have to meet anyone's timeline but your own. If you're grieving a loss, you may also feel some guilt as you move forward, fearing that you're somehow leaving your loved one behind or being selfish in your desire to move on without them. I experienced that.

Packing up the only home that John and I had shared felt like packing away our life and my memories of him for good. Of course, that couldn't have been further from what I was doing, but it still felt like a betrayal of him and our life together. What I came to understand, through counseling and self reflection, was that moving forward honored my pain, my journey, my great loss, and most of all, our love. It was a testament to the amount of love with which our home was filled and how happy we were there that it was so sad to leave it. I also knew that John wanted me to move forward, wanted me to have a happy life after he was gone.

When I met Mark and started feeling great love for him, I struggled again. Not because it meant I loved John any less (I didn't), but because Mark became the focus of my life and love and as that happened, John's big presence in my life slowly began to fade. When Mark and I got married, John's daughter Chelsey gave me a card that read "Inhale the future, exhale the past." Inside she wrote, "Today my wish for you is that you feel peace and catch your breath. Your love for Mark and his for you is exactly what dad wished you would find. Kindness and happiness. I know you'll love dad forever, but there's so much life ahead of you. I'm so happy for you." It was exactly what I needed to hear and I literally exhaled a huge sigh of relief when I read it, not realizing until that moment how much I'd been holding on and holding back, afraid to "let John go" (even though I did nothing of the sort that day). I truly believe that love expands and our capacity to love does too.

John will always be in my heart. His kids are my kids. There are photographs of him all over our home. We talk about him almost every day. I believe that is his greatest legacy and the thing that keeps him present and alive for me. I still miss him. That will never stop. I'll always love him. I believe that our relationship evolved after he died because I was willing to make a plan for my life and move forward without his physical presence in it while still holding on to everything he meant to me. He is with me every day and I will never truly let him go.

CHAPTER 20

EMBRACE
THE LEARNING

The E in the THRIVE process
stands for Embrace the Learning.

This is honestly the most simple concept in the entire process. The truth is that everything that happens in your life, every single thing, is there to teach you. Nothing is inherently "good" or "bad" except that we make it so. We assign those labels to everything that happens to us, which can hinder our ability to see and accept the learning.

That concept is simple but that doesn't make it easy. And, again, there's virtually no way you'll be able to embrace any learning for some time after a great loss. In the beginning, you'll be in too much pain to see any good in your loss. That resistance is normal and is a survival mechanism. One of the stages of grief is anger, after all, and it's difficult to ask yourself, "What has this experience taught me," when you're screaming angrily at the top of your lungs because you're in so much pain. If someone had asked me what John's death was teaching me in the first year after his death, I might have punched them dead in the face. I wasn't ready to ask that question, let alone answer it.

Eventually, however, I started to move from resistance to acceptance and that allowed me to take a bigger view of my entire journey and see that I had become a truly different person because of what I'd been through. Acceptance means understanding that everything that happens should have happened, because it did. I cannot change the past. I have no control over what has happened in my life to this point. It truly is what it is. So arguing with reality and railing about what "should" or "shouldn't" have happened will never support me. Should John have died? Obviously he should have, because he did. The only questions I can ask myself regarding that event have to do with what I can control now. *What has this taught me? Who will I be going forward because of this event? What good has come from this?*

The further away from John's death I get, the easier it is to ask (and answer) those questions. I thought my life was over when John died and I also refused to give up, knowing that what John had in store for me as I moved forward without him was worth sticking around for. He made quite a few promises in the week before he died, and he always kept his word.

In the years since his death, I've worked every day to learn, grow, evolve, and allow his loss to inform my life in a positive way, make me a better person, and create a legacy to him based on the way I choose to live. Some days I nail it, some days, not so much.

I've learned to forgive myself on the bad days and always look for the learning in every situation. Everything that happens in my life is there to teach me, and losing John has taught me more than I ever imagined it would.

I've learned to love people where they are while holding the boundaries in my own life when I need to. I've learned to let things go and forgive, for my sake—because forgiveness isn't for the person you forgive.

I've learned that most things aren't as hard as I think they are, especially when viewed through the lens of the great loss I've suffered.

I've learned not to worry about what might happen (since the things I worry about are rarely the things that come to pass). That's not always easy, but the more I can remember it, the happier I am.

I've learned that the greatest commodity in my life, the greatest gift I can give to those I love (and ask for from them as well), is time and attention. I've learned to unplug and engage a lot more often than I ever used to.

I've opened myself up to love again, taken the risk of giving my heart wholly and completely to someone new, and found great joy in that partnership in a way I never believed I would after losing John. I found someone in Mark who loves me as well and completely as John did (a miracle that I never take for granted). This was one of John's promises to me, that he'd send me the perfect person, and I will always believe he had a hand in our meeting.

I could not, in my wildest dreams, have imagined, on the day John died, all that would transpire in the coming years. That's a good thing and divinely orchestrated, I have no doubt. It keeps me present in the "now" and moving forward with the optimism of the ignorant.

I am more compassionate, with others and, more importantly, with myself. I don't let small things upset me because I understand the lack of importance they have when viewed through the lens of watching my husband starve to death in my dining room and losing the love of my life. I think I truly understand the value of the people in my life and my relationships and I invest in, and nurture them, much more carefully than I ever did before losing John. All of those things are gifts that I was given because John died. Would I change losing him if I could? Absolutely. I would have preferred to learn those life lessons in a different, less brutally painful way, but that's not what happened.

Obviously, if I had never lost John, I would never have been looking for—and consequently found—Mark. And Mark is a huge gift in my life and a daily source of joy for me. I cannot regret that I love him. It makes me think about how many times I've thought to myself, "I never should have married my kids' dad. We were not good together. That was a mistake that I regret." But then I look at my two boys, without whom I cannot imagine my life, and I know that their dad and I should have been together, because if we hadn't made that choice, I wouldn't have my boys.

Regret is a waste of time. If you find yourself experiencing it, shift to the question, "What did that teach me?" or, "What good came out of that for me?" Again, this perspective gets easier over time and is virtually inaccessible right after a painful loss. But eventually, you can choose to be grateful for the learning in any situation. If John had never gotten cancer and died, you wouldn't be reading this book because it never would have been written. My hope is that it has impacted you in some small way, that you can embrace the challenging parts of your journey, celebrate the amazing wins you'll inevitably have, give yourself grace around how you show up as you move through this time in your life, and point your sights straight at what's next. I hope that you'll look at your life and those you love from the fragile perspective of how amazing they are and how lucky you are, regardless of your circumstances. That you'll never take your life or the people in it for granted again.

Because life is truly precious and yours can change in the blink of an eye. The key, my friend, is how aware you are of that fact and how you choose to move through your life regardless of what comes your way. Trust me when I tell you, you can move on from anything. It may take time and you may have to fight your way through it, but it's worth the fight when you come out the other side, look around, and realize you're thriving.

CHAPTER 21

#LIVELIKEJOHNNY

As we end our journey together, it's important to me that we do so looking forward. To that end, I'd like to share something I did the day after John died that created a small movement. It's my hope that this book will help this movement grow, because that would be the greatest legacy I could ever create out of John's death.

As I blogged through the two-and-a-half years of John's cancer and the years after he died, I used the hashtag #Lovetrumpscancer. As I've said in this book, we always believed that the only way to truly "beat" terminal cancer was to focus on love, and that hashtag became the rallying cry for us and my followers. The day after John died my sister Melissa wrote a beautiful tribute to him on Facebook. She spoke about his life, the difference he had made in my life, and the impact he had on our entire family. She shared how his love had changed me and what an incredible human he was. I read that post and suddenly realized that it was time for a new hashtag. I posted the following on Facebook on February 8th, 2016, the day after John died.

Julie Kick
Feb 8, 2016

Something my sister Melissa wrote in her beautiful tribute to my amazing Johnny this morning made me realize that we need a new hashtag now that he's won his battle and cancer has lost. She talked about how positive he was, always, no matter what was going on in his body or how much pain he was in. She talked about that big, ever-present smile that could light up a room and how he was always concerned about everyone around him. He never sweated the small stuff. He was, simply, the most happy, positive person I've ever met.

The greatest tribute to him is the thousands of messages I've received in the past few years from people telling us how much our journey has inspired and changed their lives, telling us that they are living their lives differently or appreciating their loved ones

more because of how John lived and how
we took this journey together.

So let's start spreading the hashtag
#livelikeJohnny. Any time you feel inspired
by our journey or you think of him and smile
because of who he was or how he touched
your life, share that and use the hashtag.
Any time you live in the moment and life
is wonderful and you feel happy, use
the hashtag.

John was a giver. Doing things for and
making a difference in the lives of others
was what drove him, 100%. Making that
hashtag go viral would be the greatest
legacy he could leave, and the one that
would make him the most happy. Let's all
choose to #livelikeJohnny and spread that
love whenever possible.

Where in your life are you "living like Johnny" and how does
it impact you when you choose to do that? What if you made
a conscious decision to choose joy more often? To look for the
love and learning in difficult situations and relationships? I
can tell you from experience, it can make a bad day better and
a good day fabulous. If you're a person who shares on social
media, I'd love to invite you to use the #livelikeJohnny hashtag
and allow it to remind you of how blessed you are. My hope is,
with the context of this book and our story, you'll understand
that #livelikeJohnny gives you a chance to celebrate life and

choose to focus on the good, no matter what's happening in your life.

Writing this book has truly been a labor of love for me. As I said in the introduction, the reason it took me almost five years to complete was because, just like labor, it was painful and hard. I'm honored that you chose to read it and it's my fervent hope that you're taking some inspiration from that experience and that my story and the THRIVE process will have a huge impact on your life.

I love to hear from my readers and would be honored to have you reach out to share your own story of how the book impacted you. You can find me at Julie@weatheringthegriefstorm.com or www.weatheringthegriefstorm.com. If you enjoyed this book, I'd consider it a personal favor if you headed over to Amazon and wrote a review. I'm looking forward to hearing from you!

ACKNOWLEDGEMENTS

To John's kids, my step-kids Chelsey and Chad, for willingly welcoming me as your step-mom all those years ago, and for keeping me as family after John died. You two are the children of my heart and could not feel more like mine if I'd given birth to you. You were your dad's treasures and the greatest gift he ever gave me. And to Chelsey, for creating the website for the book and giving me invaluable feedback as it came to life.

To my youngest son Eli, who was the only other person who lived through the daily struggle of John's cancer battle and my struggle to survive after his death. Your quiet strength and compassion never cease to amaze me my beautiful boy, and I am blessed by you, as was John. He would have been proud of the man you have become.

To my eldest son Sam, the bringer of joy in my life (even when you exasperate me), for helping me remember to always stay present, because you're the most happy, present person I've ever known.

To my husband Mark, the next great love of my life, for loving me through anything and being content to let me love John too. So much of me coming back to life happened once I met you and my life would not be the happy place it has become without you.

To my family (my mom Joy, my sister Melissa and her family, and my brothers Jeff and Mark and their families), for being there for me and holding me up, for giving me a safe place to land when I needed it, and for making John and his kids part of our family.

To my best friend since high school Kate Myre-Graham, for knowing me so well, showing up when I need you most, and making me laugh until I pee my pants. You and your family were my happy place during the worst time in my life, and I love you all.

To my kids' dad David Gentzler, his wife Valerie, and his mom Carol, for wrapping your arms around us before John died and for reminding me that family is family, no matter what, after he died. I will never forget your kindness.

To the Pride of Portland Sweet Adelines Chorus and our former director Ryan Heller, for your love and support, and for being the one place I could go each week to escape the sadness in my life and sing. You provided some of the best therapy I had before and after John died.

To Jim House, "The Book Carver" (and my friend), for helping me find the THRIVE process within my story.

To my Facebook friends and followers, most of whom I've never met, who gave me so much support and prayed thousands and thousands of prayers for John, me, and our family over the course of his illness and after he died. You will never know what a positive impact you had.

To the staff at Walla Walla Community Hospice, for your gentle, kind support at the end of John's life and, more importantly, during the beginning of my grieving process. I'm pretty sure you saved my life.

To Dr. John Thompson from Seattle Cancer Care Alliance in Seattle, Washington, for your compassion, expertise, and excellent care during John's entire cancer journey, and for the personal phone call and your kind words when you learned of his passing.

To the nursing staff at the infusion center at Providence St. Mary's Medical Center in Walla Walla, Washington, for making every visit brighter, always having a smile for us, and your presence at John's memorial service. He adored each and every one of you and you made his difficult journey easier.

ABOUT THE AUTHOR

Julie Kick is an ICF Accredited life and business coach, trainer, and keynote speaker. Known as "the Systems Specialist," she can break down just about any concept or big picture problem into doable steps. Her training topics include personal development, coaching and mentoring skills, leadership skills, and using the THRIVE process during life after loss. She has been writing her entire life but this is her first book.

In February of 2016 Julie's husband and soulmate lost his battle with cancer. His death and working through the grieving process has taught her the value of each moment and inspired her to share her experience and the lessons she's learned with her audiences and in this book.

Julie lives with her husband Mark in Vancouver, Washington. She has two grown boys, three grown step-children, and two grandchildren.

CPSIA information can be obtained
at www.ICGtesting.com
Printed in the USA
BVHW031137120421
604740BV00001B/9

9 781949 635928